ROGER WILLIAMS UNIVERSITY LIBRARY

3 1931 00377 6241

CURRICULUM MATERIALS CENTER

Creating Writers in the Primary Classroom

D1372668

ROGER WILLIAMS UNIV. LIBRARY

Creating Writers in the Primary Classroom

Practical approaches to inspire teachers and their pupils

Miles Tandy
and
Jo Howell

Routledge
Taylor & Francis Group

LONDON AND NEW YORK

CURRICULUM MATERIALS CENTER

CMC
LB
1576
.T24
2008

181335798

4/09

First published 2008
by Routledge
2 Park Square, Milton Park, Abingdon, Oxon OX14 4RN

Simultaneously published in the USA and Canada
by Routledge
270 Madison Avenue, New York, NY 10016

Routledge is an imprint of the Taylor & Francis Group, an informa business

© 2008 Miles Tandy and Jo Howell

Typeset in Goudy and Trade Gothic by RefineCatch Limited, Bungay, Suffolk
Printed and bound in Great Britain by Antony Rowe Ltd, Chippenham, Wiltshire

All rights reserved. No part of this book may be reprinted or reproduced or utilised in any form or by any electronic, mechanical, or other means, now known or hereafter invented, including photocopying and recording, or in any information storage or retrieval system, without permission in writing from the publishers.

British Library Cataloguing in Publication Data
A catalogue record for this book is available from the British Library

Library of Congress Cataloging-in-Publication Data
Tandy, Miles.
 Creating writers in the primary classroom: practical approaches to inspire teachers and their pupils/Miles Tandy and Jo Howell.
   p. cm.
 1. English language – Composition and exercises – Study and teaching (Elementary) – Great Britain. 2. Creative writing (Elementary education) – Great Britain. I. Howell, Jo., 1972– . II. Title.
 LB1576.T24 2008
 372.62′3–dc22   2007046125

ISBN 10: 0-415-45267-8 (pbk)
ISBN 10: 0-203-92743-5 (ebk)

ISBN 13: 978-0-415-45267-0 (pbk)
ISBN 13: 978-0-203-92743-4 (ebk)

CMC LB1576 .T24 2008
Tandy, Miles
Creating writers in the
primary classroom :
practical approaches to
inspire teachers and their
pupils

 # Contents

Foreword

An art and a craft and a marvellous magic

A certain fear of the empty page has stayed with me since my schooldays. For me it still seems perfectly to mirror an empty mind bereft of ideas. It saps my confidence and my will and any hope I might be harbouring that I can cover the page with words at all, let alone with a coherent story. Yet, almost every day of my life, I choose to face down that fear. It is not because I am brave. Rather I am like a sailor who knows the terror of the seas and has discovered over the years and after countless voyages and adventures that the only way to banish this terror is by knowing and understanding the sea in all its moods so well that he is no longer frustrated when becalmed, nor terrified for his life in the midst of the storm. And just as a sailor goes out once again to face the perils of the open sea, so I go to my bed each day, pile up my pillows behind me, settle back, pick up a pen, drawn up my knees, open the exercise book and confront once more the open sea of the empty page. The mariner sails the sea because he longs to, because it is a challenge he needs, because each time he is testing himself, exploring, discovering. I write for the same reasons.

But my need to write has another motivation too, one I share in part at least with sailors, I think. I like to feel connected, to myself, to my memory, to the world about me, to my readers. It is, I suppose, my way of feeling most intensely that I belong.

I have often wondered in four decades of writing how it is that time and again my stories seem to gather themselves, write themselves almost (the best ones really seem to), cover the empty pages almost effortlessly – once I get going, that is. Each one is, I believe, the result of forces of a creative fusion, a fusion that simply can't happen unless certain elements are in place, a fusion I don't properly understand, but can only guess at. But it is an informed guess.

At the core of it, without which there would simply never have been any fusion at all, is the life I have lived: as a child in London, as a son and a brother on the Essex coast, away at boarding school, then as a soldier, a student, a husband, a father, a teacher, farmer, traveller, lecturer, storyteller, grandfather. I didn't live this life in order to write stories, of course – for at least half of my life I had no idea I even wanted to write – but without its joys and its pain, its highs and its lows, I would have precious little to write about and probably no desire to write anyway.

For me, memory is the source material that is needed for this fusion – the memory of falling off a bike into a ditch ('Singing for Mrs Pettigrew'); of being a castaway on an island in Scilly (*Why the Whales Came*; *Kensuke's Kingdom*); of collecting cowrie shells on a beach near Zennor ('The Giant's Necklace'); of running away from boarding school (*The Butterfly Lion*; 'My One and Only Great Escape'); of a family friend terribly scarred when he was shot down in the RAF in the war ('Half a Man'); of seeing my father for the first time in my life ('My Father Is a Polar Bear'); of loving the paintings of Cézanne (*Meeting Cézanne*) and the music of Mozart, the poetry of Ted Hughes (*The Silver Swan*) and the stories of Robert Louis Stevenson (*I Believe in Unicorns*); of a small boy sitting on his tricycle in a square in Venice at ten o'clock at night watching a violinist play in the street ('The Mozart Question'); of a village divided over the construction of an atomic power station; of a lady who lived in a railway carriage near the sea and gave me a glass of milk and a jam sandwich when I was little; and of a single lark rising into the blue (*Singing for Mrs Pettigrew*). So it is no accident that every one of these things has made its way later into a story of mine.

But memories themselves are not enough to create the fusion that fires a story. To have read widely and deeply, to have soaked oneself in the words and ideas of other writers, to have seen what is possible and wonderful, to have listened to the music of their words and to have read the work of the masters must be a help for any writer discovering his own technique, her own voice.

My own writing has taken all my years to develop – is still developing, I hope – and it has happened in parallel with my life and my reading. Once the spark is there – and with me the spark is always the result of some fusion between events I have lived or witnessed or discovered – then comes the time for research, and with research a growing confidence that I have the wherewithal to write it and then a conviction that I have a burning need to write it.

But I must wait for the moment before I begin (procrastination has its uses!), until the story is ripe. This process can be five minutes (unlikely) or five years. All I know is that you can't hurry it. The story will be written when the moment is right. I learned some time ago not to force the pace, not to dictate the story but to allow the story time to find its own voice to weave itself, to dream itself out in my head so that, by the time I set pen to paper, I feel I am living inside that story. I must know the places; I must know the people. I may still not know exactly what will happen – and certainly not how it might end. That often emerges through the writing. But I do know by now the world of my story intimately, its tone and tune, its cadence and rhythm. I feel I am living inside it, that even as I am writing about it I am not the creator of it at all, but simply telling it as it happens, as I witness it. And when it's written, I read it over, to hear the music of it in my head, to be sure the tune and the story are in harmony. No note must jar, or the dream of the story is interrupted.

The last and most important element in the alchemy that produces this creative fusion is the sheer love of doing it, of seeing if you can make magic from an empty page and a pen. The truth is that it is not a trick. It is an art and a craft and a marvellous magic, and I long with every story to understand it better and to do it better too.

Michael Morpurgo
First published in
Singing for Mrs Pettigrew,
Walker Books, 2006

Dedicated to the memory of Jackie Page 1946–2006: headteacher; mentor; friend.

Acknowledgements

We should like to thank all our colleagues at the Educational Development Service in Warwickshire for their support, particularly Lyn Johnson and Barbara Brown whose influence has been profound. Thanks also to all the Warwickshire teachers and children with whom we have worked, particularly those at Kineton C of E Primary School and Shustoke C of E Primary School. Thanks to Thomas and Ryan for their wonderful writing, and to Denise and Gideon for their patience and support throughout.

Something worth writing about?

Introduction

Teaching children to write can be exceptionally rewarding work. If you have been close at hand while young writers find a voice that is uniquely theirs and begin their early mastery of the written word, then you are fortunate indeed. Writing at its best is a powerful medium: it allows us to recount experiences, real or imagined; to express our thoughts, feelings and ideas; to argue, advocate and persuade. As they learn to do these things, children grow to think how writers think, to feel how writers feel, to experience what writers experience, and to write how writers write. And good writing can change things for the better: we need only to think of the power of a good letter of application or a well-written complaint; either can have an immediate and sometimes dramatic effect on our lives. For those lucky enough to be shown how to do it, there is true delight to be had in that sense of achievement and fulfilment which comes from knowing that one has written something and written it well. To leave children unable to write, more particularly unable to write well, can have a direct and damaging effect on the options that might be open to them in their adult lives.

Small wonder then, that the teaching of writing in our schools has been given such high priority in recent years. In England, it would not be exaggerating to say that our teaching has gone through something of a revolution. The practices of modelling for, sharing with and guiding children to help them become confident, independent writers are very much more widespread than they were a decade ago. In many schools, they are so firmly embedded that they are a natural part of our daily teaching. These are practices which attend explicitly to the skills of the writer and show children how writing is made. And we should applaud them and all the teachers who have worked so hard to sustain them in their regular teaching practice.

And yet there seem to be so many primary schools in which the teaching of writing remains a significant issue and area for development. Whether it is through national test results, inspection by the Office for Standards in Education, or a school's own careful assessment and analysis of children's written work, many identify improving children's writing as a major concern. For many teachers and school leaders this can be frustrating to the point of exasperation: after all, they have worked *so* hard at implementing the recommended strategies, at planning, at marking and assessing. And still there seems to be something missing.

We speak to a great many teachers in the course of our work and most of them identify a very similar set of issues and problems in relation to writing in their schools. For all the hard work that has gone into addressing it in recent years, spelling persists as a challenge to many young writers. Even when they manage to spell difficult words in the lessons we have devoted to teaching it, getting correct spelling to be a natural part of independent writing is a challenge of an entirely different order. We are all very well aware of how a lack of confidence in his ability to spell can affect a young writer's willingness to write. Then teachers often talk of children's limited experience, often of their limited vocabulary, and often of a perceived connection between the two. A lack of imagination is also widely identified: why do they seem to have so few and such limited ideas? All these factors combine to give rise to that most familiar of cries, 'I don't know what to write!' And we have all worked *so* hard.

This gentle parody might serve to illustrate something of the problem:

Remembering to open some sentences with a subordinate clause, the young writer dutifully began. It was a warm, sunlit afternoon and the stuffy room was filled with his classmates, all eager to show off their hard-earned skills.

'That last sentence was impressively long,' he thought to himself, 'But I may have used a few too many commas.' He knew very well that he must show his command of a range of punctuation: colons; semi-colons; even dashes – if only he could find a way to work some of those in.

'Stop!' he could almost hear his teacher cry. 'Remember what we've been talking about: think of your reader.' And she was right. Perhaps it was time to ask a question to draw his reader in? Should he add some shorter sentences to help build tension?

This writer knew all about tension. Palms sweating, he remembered the dramatic effect of short sentences. Very short. Tiny. If the passive voice was used for the next sentence, the tension would become almost unbearable. Who had written that last one? And why?

There could be no doubt about it: this was a writer who could really see the craft.

continued

'Look, look!' they cried. 'There's the craft!' I could see the craft and it was bright and shiny with all lights on it and it was full of aliens and they came towards me and there was a big fight.

'POW! POW! POW!' I shot them with my laser gun and I killed them all until they are all dead and the end.

Perhaps it is a little unkind but, as you will have guessed right away, no real writer ever wrote it. Yet the problem it illustrates will be familiar to many teachers: there is so much more to effective and engaging writing than the slavish application of technique. What we have all learned to call 'the craft of the writer' is about much more than remembering all the 'tricks of the trade'; speak to most writers and they will tell you that there are very few of those. What is more, when we become overly concerned with such techniques it can easily make our writing tiresomely self-conscious: at best laboured and labouring; at worst just plain clichéd. And when the young writer imagined in this piece suddenly finds a story raging in his head like a film or a video game, that frail veneer of technique quickly deserts him. All of which begs the question: What *does* make a good writer and what *is* good writing?

Once we have written something and given it up to the reader, the words are everything. Sometimes they may interact subtly and beautifully with illustrations, photographs, sounds or even video. Even then, what we write has to stand alone and do its own work: the writer is not generally on hand to explain, interpret or correct. Yet good writing can entertain, inspire, illuminate, clarify, and sometimes even move the reader to tears. We know that such writing has real 'depth' to it: a depth of experience, of feeling, and of subtle skill. In many ways the words that appear on the page are only 'the tip of an iceberg'. The iceberg is a widely used metaphor and we are all familiar with the idea that the greater part of it lies beneath the surface, mostly out of sight. We want to use that familiar image to propose a model of how we might rethink what makes children good writers and how we can all help them to get better.

The iceberg model

The 'iceberg' model we propose (see Figure 1.1) builds through four stages to offer some analysis of what might be needed to make a writer, and then suggests a number of headings under which a school can take deliberate and planned action to create that writer in every child.

When a child (or anyone for that matter) writes, the words we see on the page are all we have. Whether we read them as a teacher, a parent, another child, or even an external examiner of writing tests, we have only what we can see to celebrate, judge, applaud, criticise, or simply enjoy. And when we see those words, we can apply very particular

- Handwriting
- Spelling
- Punctuation
- Vocabulary

The words
on the page

- Text structure
- Sentence construction
- Cohesion

?

Figure 1.1 The words on the page as the 'tip of the iceberg'

criteria to judge them and maybe even assign them a level according to the National Curriculum. Young writers are regularly judged in this way. We should be very clear that the skills and abilities that are so judged are vital and that nothing we say is intended to detract in any way from the importance of teaching them. We have placed these skills 'above the surface' in our model because they are the most readily seen, often the most straightforward to judge, and often appear to be the most 'teachable'.

We suggest that it is in the teaching of these very 'visible' writer's skills – spelling and handwriting, vocabulary, punctuation and grammar, text structure and cohesion – that the dramatic changes in practice of recent years have been most evident. There has been a strong emphasis on assessing and analysing what appears on the page when children write, identifying those elements of the visible skills which need developing, and focusing our teaching very deliberately on those. We may, for instance, discover through our analysis of assessments that children seem to have a particular problem with unstressed vowels in polysyllabic words. As a result of this we can develop clear strategies to address the perceived problem and conduct further assessments at a later date to judge how much difference our teaching has made. For addressing particular technical writing skills, this approach can be highly effective.

If we pursue the metaphor of the iceberg further though, it may reveal another problem which is so often experienced by the teachers with whom we work. However big or small an iceberg might be, the proportions above and below the surface will remain constant at about one-ninth above and eight-ninths below. So if we were to try to increase the size of a real iceberg just by adding more and more ice above the surface, eight-ninths of it will sink out of sight. Keep doing this for too long and the iceberg would probably become unstable and capsize. So what might happen with the metaphorical iceberg of children's writing? Many teachers can relate to the experience of working away at particular sets of skills, for example, spelling, finding that children complete all their exercises and worksheets accurately only to see those skills disappear when they are asked to write independently. Perhaps they have 'sunk' below the surface? We suggest that if you want more significant and sustainable improvement in what appears on the page, improvement that is appreciated not only by you the teacher but by the writers themselves, you may also need to look a little further and deeper at what lies beneath the surface.

The importance of experience

In *Dear Mr Morpingo*, Geoff Fox takes us 'inside the world' of the children's writer Michael Morpurgo. He tells us that almost every time the writer gives a talk in school, Michael is asked the same question: 'Where do you get your ideas from, Mr Morpurgo?' That question is a very good one. How is it possible for one man to produce such an extraordinary range of such high-quality writing? Is it because his spelling is so exceptional, or that he has particularly beautiful and fluent handwriting? Both may be true, but what is clear is that the answer to the question 'Where do you get your ideas from?' is as complex and difficult to fathom for Michael Morpurgo as it is for any other writer. We suggest that much of the answer lies beneath the surface and may not be so easily visible (see Figure 1.2).

When we write, we draw on experience, and we need more than just our technical skills. Our ability, enthusiasm and inspiration to write will be profoundly affected by where we've been, what we've seen, heard, touched, felt, smelled, or even tasted. What have I read? What have I thought and imagined? And how am I personally affected by all these

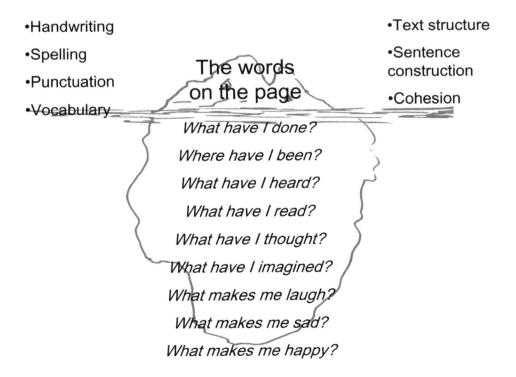

Figure 1.2 What lies beneath the surface?

experiences? What makes me happy or sad, moves me to laughter or tears, makes me hopeful or despondent? The answers to those questions are importantly different for all of us and yet, we suggest, can have a profound effect on the writer we might each become.

We suggest that a richness and diversity of these experiences encourages the development of another set of writer's skills (see Figure 1.3): less visible on the page, less technical and less obviously 'teachable', but certainly no less important.

Writers need to look, listen, feel, smell and taste. And when they do all those things, they need to *notice*. So many good writers have an eye – or an ear or a nose – for detail. It is so often in the noticing of such detail, and the skilful use of it in their writing, that they are able to share experiences with us and draw us as readers into them. Good writers can not only paint a grand landscape in words, they can also draw our attention to some tiny detail that evokes a time, a place or a person with extraordinary clarity. When they hear, it is not only the everyday sounds that are all around us; it is also the particular and delightful details of the ways people really speak to each other. They notice how people look or don't look at each other when they are talking, how the ways in which they sit or stand or move all give us clues about what they are thinking and feeling.

The widespread use of the term 'creative writing', most usually applied to fiction and poetry, can easily lead us to forget that *all* writing is, in essence, a creative process. Until we write, there is nothing on the page and whatever finishes up there has been *created* by the writer. Creating is fundamentally about making, about fashioning, shaping and

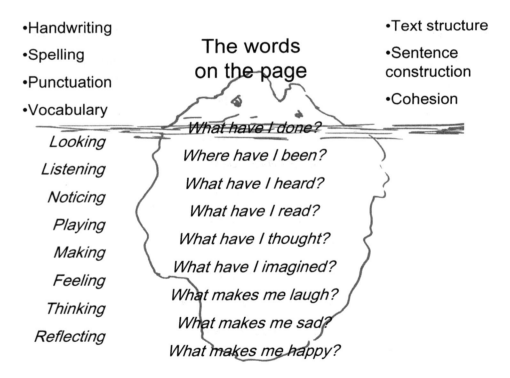

Figure 1.3 Some other writers' skills?

crafting. But creating can also be a playful process and good writers may be very playful. This is not just about a willingness to be inventive with words on the page, important though that is. It is also about the vital relationship between play and imagination. In their role play, young children are capable of creating and sustaining imagined worlds and living out stories in the world they have made, be that world a home, a shop, a magic castle, or even another planet. In essence it is the same capacity as that shown by Philip Pullman in the remarkable *His Dark Materials* trilogy. Entire worlds are invented and given life with extraordinary consistency.

The last sets of skills we identify are those of thinking, feeling and reflecting. In many ways these present the greatest challenge to our practice and to current educational orthodoxies. Thinking, feeling and reflecting need time and space, both of which are difficult to find in many primary schools. They are not always driven by objectives and their effects cannot always be seen in children's writing the day after tomorrow. But most writers know just how important it can be to take time, to let ideas take root and grow, and to return to them more than once. There is a very understandable temptation to believe that the best way to learn to write a complete piece in under an hour is through repeated, timed practice. In order to prepare children to face that ordeal, some practice of this kind may be helpful, but it is never going to create writers. Take time to develop children fully as writers, we suggest, and they will perform well in any test anyone chooses to give them. If we teach them to take tests, they might also perform well, but they will never make writers.

When we use the iceberg model during our in-service work with teachers, it is generally recognised and accepted as a clear way of analysing a particular problem. Like all such models, of course, it is deceptively simple. Though we have tried to outline them as clearly as we can, the experience and skills that lie 'beneath the surface' for a writer are very complex and subtly different for every young writer we teach. And if the iceberg metaphor holds, something like eight-ninths of what makes a writer lies in this murky, sub-surface domain. Many teachers are also quick to recognise how much the experience and subtle range of skills that lie beneath the surface will vary not just from one child to another, but from one school to another. Many feel that their children are at a distinct disadvantage from the start. Some will arrive at school with a glorious richness and diversity of experiences, a growing love of literature that has been devotedly nurtured in them by their parents since they were tiny, and an imagination that surprises and delights us with its capacity to play, invent and create. Other children seem to have rather less. At that point some teachers might be forgiven for throwing up their hands in despair and lamenting the unfairness of it all, the crude brutality of league tables and the failure of those in power to realise the struggle that we face. But to their enormous credit, most teachers remain very positive and are eager to explore what they might begin to do about it all. That is what this book is fundamentally about. Those capacities teachers have developed for the deliberate and focused teaching of particular writing skills remain essential and we show how you can keep right on using them. But this is not another book about how to teach spelling or handwriting or grammar or how to

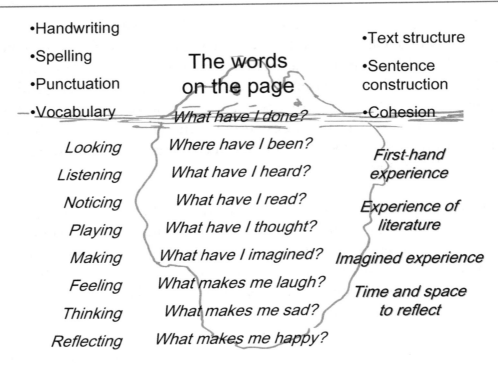

- •Handwriting
- •Spelling
- •Punctuation
- •Vocabulary

The words
on the page

- •Text structure
- •Sentence construction
- •Cohesion

What have I done?

Looking	*Where have I been?*	*First-hand experience*
Listening	*What have I heard?*	
Noticing	*What have I read?*	*Experience of literature*
Playing	*What have I thought?*	
Making	*What have I imagined?*	*Imagined experience*
Feeling	*What makes me laugh?*	*Time and space to reflect*
Thinking	*What makes me sad?*	
Reflecting	*What makes me happy?*	

Figure 1.4 Four essential elements

recognise and write different non-fiction text types. There are plenty of those on the market and many teachers have also benefited from a good deal of in-service work to address those very particular teaching skills. Our central concern is to introduce and illustrate some teaching approaches that build on the essential writing capacities that lie beneath the surface, that are harder to see, perhaps more subtle to teach, but no less vital in the development of young writers. Equally, we address very particular and practical teaching strategies which help the young writers' experience to 'break the surface' so that when they write they are able to draw on all they know, have experienced, what they think and what they feel. In taking this approach, we suggest there are four essential elements (see Figure 1.4).

First-hand experience

Ask a good teacher of the early years – or any good teacher for that matter – and they will tell you just how vital first-hand experience is for all learning. If a richness of experience is essential for a writer, then it has to be gained at first hand and we need to bring all our senses to the process. This may seem obvious, but it is not always easy to do if we feel that time is so precious and pressured. Some developments in recent years seem to have resulted in primary school children spending more and more time in their classrooms, sitting at their desks. And when they do get out of the classroom, we are often so determined to meet our learning objectives that we give them little time to look and listen, touch, feel and smell what is around them. This is not to suggest that the first-hand experiences we offer to children should be unstructured or woolly, rather that we might think more deeply about how we draw on them *with* the children. First-hand experience is something that you have, not something that is packaged and given to you.

Early years teachers can really lead the way here. A group of teachers who work mainly with older children came together at one of their schools for an in-service day at which we wanted to explore how we might use the outdoors and the local area to develop children's writing. It was a gruesome day with near-horizontal rain in the bitter wind. As we arrived, soaking and uncomfortable, we all wondered about the wisdom of getting outside as we had planned. When we saw the Reception class togged up in coats, hats and scarves and going about their outdoor play as usual, we all felt shamed into getting out there too. And yes, it was cold and wet. But we saw it, felt it and heard it. How often do we expect children to write about a stormy night when they've never really experienced even a stormy day? If you've never experienced any such thing, what can you do but fall back on tired clichés about howling winds and driving rain? We really need to get out more.

Of course we can have good-quality first-hand experiences in the classroom too. Things that we can touch and feel, smell and sometimes taste can all be part of our daily experiences. Trying on clothes, for example, or using historical artefacts can significantly deepen our engagement with them. Not only might such experiences have a direct and immediate impact on what we write and how, they also become part of a 'bank' of experience on which we might draw, sometimes unexpectedly, at a much later time.

Experience of literature

It is common enough to find an avid reader who does not write much, but very rare to find a writer who does not read. Good writers tend to read good books. They are generally members of a community of readers who sometimes read books alone, sometimes read them together, sometimes read them in silence, sometimes read them aloud. They talk about the books they have read, listen to what others have to say about them, argue, challenge, laugh and sometimes cry about them. But they read and read.

For a school to be a place where writing flourishes, it also needs to have a widespread culture of reading. Reading is something that is celebrated everywhere: in the classrooms; in the library; in the displays around the school; in the staffroom; in assemblies; at the book fair; with all the children and with all their families. Everyone loves books. It seems, then, a particularly bizarre consequence of a National Literacy Strategy in England that many teachers seem to spend less time reading aloud to children than they did before it was introduced. Often this is because of an understandable fear of some hapless soul with a clipboard asking the teacher what their objectives are. Reading aloud to children just for the sheer joy of doing it should be part of the daily experience every good school offers and we should all fight to keep it so. There can be few better ways of engendering a love of books, a love of stories, and a true delight in the written word.

We also know that good books provide children with models of what good writing might look like. We can show them how the book is structured, explore how the writer achieves particular effects, and speculate why she might have made particular choices. All these practices are good and mostly well embedded. What is equally important though is that they build on that firm foundation of a school-wide reading culture. Children's close analysis of a text should, when done well, help them to love books all the more. Done badly and slavishly it seems to have quite the opposite effect.

With several thousand children's books published every year there are plenty from which to choose. Since no school has a limitless budget to spend on books, it is essential that we spend what money we have very wisely. This necessitates us making judgements of value and teaching children to do the same. In all those thousands, there are some terrific books that should be in every school in the country. The best books take the reader into other worlds and, for a time, can lose them there. The commonly used phrase 'lost in a book' captures something of what can happen to a lucky reader. If a writer has written her story well, the reader is led into a world that is partly created by the writer; partly in the reader's imagination. In doing so, the reader is able to imagine experiences that they could not otherwise have. The good writer can introduce us to people who seem as real as anyone we have ever met, give us the sensation of having visited places we have never seen, and help us to imagine all sorts of experiences that we might be too cautious, too fearful, too lucky, or perhaps too poor to experience for ourselves. Those experiences build and build below the writer's surface skills and strengthen the reserves they have to draw on when they write. Good books matter and good writers read lots of them.

Imagined experience

In many ways, reading a book might be described as an 'imagined experience', and in the best books it can feel very real indeed. But there are other ways in which we can help children to imagine the experience of other people in other places and at other times. Such experiences can be invaluable when they write.

For most children their imagined experiences start very young in something we call play. This may be referred to as role play or imaginative play. What characterises it is the capacity of children to suspend the normal rules of time, place and identity and be others at other times and in other places. Two children may decide that they are going to be a mum and a dad: a doll or another toy may be chosen to be their child. It is worth noticing that they don't so much *pretend* to be the mum and dad as *be* them, and for however long they choose to sustain their play, they try on the roles of mum and dad. In the world of their imaginations they have *been* mum and dad, thought how mums and dads think and felt how mums and dads feel. As they get older these kinds of experiences may be structured differently for and with children through the medium of drama. Through that highly versatile medium, skilled teachers can help children to imagine the experience of a journey to the South Pole, of desertion on a lonely island, or of serving as a Roman soldier on Hadrian's Wall. Play, drama and theatre are essentially processes through which we imagine together and this makes them highly effective means through which we can actively teach children how to imagine. As such they have a vital and unique contribution to building that essential depth of writers' experience.

Though some teachers we speak to may find it a little uncomfortable, children have other sources of imagined experience too. It is very tempting to dismiss the value of film, television and video games, but for many young writers they are a very significant source of stories. Like play, drama and theatre, film and television also create imagined worlds in which the viewer can become completely absorbed. They can provide important and valuable subjects for discussion and analysis. As the technology becomes much more widely available, there are also important opportunities for children to create, not just consume these media. Adults may be all too ready to dismiss them as unimaginative, but in some of the best video games the young player is a very active agent in the story that unfolds on the screen. What he does and how he chooses to act influence what happens and may require much more imagination than we sometimes care to admit.

Time and space to reflect

As we have already suggested, this can be one of the hardest elements of the writer's practice to build into the primary curriculum. 'Pace' has become one of the most tyrannical words in the educational lexicon in recent years and it can sometimes make teachers fearful of allowing children the time and space to think, reflect and let their ideas grow. Yet if what lies beneath the surface of the writer's iceberg is to have real strength and depth, such time and space are essential.

Good writing is often the result of long, hard and careful thought. In some instances this thinking will start some time before a word appears on the page. Even when the writing process has begun and the first words appear, many writers will tell you how important it is to break from what they are doing, think, rethink and reflect. Any teacher might reasonably respond to this by pointing out that, in England at least, children's writing is publicly assessed when they have no such time available to them: they have a very short time in which to conceive and execute a piece of writing which is expected to show the very best of what they can do. Whatever any of us might think of that process, it is still the reality that children and their teachers face. What, that teacher might ask, is the point of giving them the advantage of a rich and extended experience of the writing process when they will have no such luxury when they are tested? We can only respond by saying that good and confident writers will perform very much better in any test anyone chooses to give them than will poor ones who lack confidence and belief in themselves as writers.

The practice we outline and illustrate in subsequent chapters shows how the time and space to reflect is one element in a rich and varied dynamic of teaching and learning. There are times when ideas for writing may be generated very quickly, spontaneously and playfully; others where we all need to get our heads down and work hard at getting the words on to the page; and other times when a slower, more reflective tempo may be just what is needed. What is most important is that teachers and learners work together to orchestrate these elements of pace over time so that they combine to enable the best possible writing from everyone.

A sense of audience

Most teachers are very familiar with the importance of audience and purpose for children's writing. We often teach children that the people for whom we are writing and what we are trying to do for them should determine the form of writing that we choose. But if the young writer's depth of experience is to 'break the surface' in the way we describe, that audience needs to feel – and be – as real as possible. 'Let's imagine we're writing a letter of complaint' is very different from, 'let's write and complain about that then'. The audience for children's writing needs to be wider than just their teacher sitting at home and marking their books. As we will show, children need to be active in deciding who those audiences are. If, as a young writer, I am going to apply all my skills with enthusiasm and commitment, then I need to know that the writing I am bringing into the world will be of interest to someone. I need to know that what lies beneath the surface of my iceberg is worth the effort required to get it above. A clear sense of a real audience can greatly raise writers' expectations of themselves.

Finding the time to teach it all

Only one-ninth of an iceberg is visible above the water; the other eight-ninths are below the surface and mostly out of sight. A teacher could very reasonably look at the model we have offered and conclude that eight out of every nine writing lessons should be given over to developing the sub-surface skills and experiences which we have outlined, and only one out of nine devoted to teaching those more visible skills of spelling, handwriting, punctuation, etc. Most would feel, quite rightly, that that would not be a sensible course of action. While we show that understanding the iceberg model has clear implications for what happens during your writing lessons, we also demonstrate how the model might have an impact right across the primary curriculum. Good schools keep their curriculum under review and when we have used this model with them, it has often provoked teachers to ask some searching questions about the quality of experiences which are offered through their whole curriculum. The English curriculum, however good and rich it may be, cannot do all of this on its own. It is not a bad question to ask of almost any aspect of your curriculum: What is this doing to build children's depth and richness of experience? This is not to suggest that all your curriculum time should be given over to the teaching of writing. But building in as many rich experiences as we can, making the best possible use of the school grounds, the local area and visits further afield, planning imagined experience into as many areas of the curriculum as we can, and building in time for thought and reflection, all help to build up that depth of experience which writers need. If you think of the curriculum in this way, we suggest that the quality and depth of learning and experience in all subjects and areas can only benefit. A school where the curriculum has richness and diversity built into it will create good writers and many of the examples we offer in this book show that principle in action.

A renewed Primary Framework for literacy

For almost a decade the teaching of writing in English primary schools has been dominated by the *National Literacy Strategy Framework for Teaching*. It sets out clear learning objectives for the teaching of reading and writing, term by term and year by year as children progress through primary school. In 2006 a renewed *Primary Framework for literacy and mathematics* was published and distributed to all English primary schools. There are some significant changes in approach which underpin the renewed framework, which you will find developed and extended through this book.

The renewed framework includes specific reference to speaking and listening: it is integrated into the framework with a clear model of progression. In all the approaches we outline, we emphasise the fundamental importance of speaking and listening as the foundation on which writing is built. This cannot be over-emphasised and you will hear it echo right through everything we do.

The framework also encourages teachers to think and plan in units of work of two, three or four weeks. We are encouraged to plan these units in such a way that children's skills and understanding develop over a period of time through the cycle of review, teach, practise, apply, and evaluate. We illustrate that essential cycle and show how it can culminate in children producing outcomes which not only demonstrate and celebrate the skills they are acquiring, but bring them to completed pieces of writing in which they can take genuine pride. Integral to this approach is the kind of pragmatic, practical and productive planning which we outline in Chapter 7. Assessment for learning lies at its heart – understanding where the children are in their development as writers and what they might need from us next. The flexibility and responsiveness which is integral to this approach is carefully illustrated, as is the subtle and delicate balance between teacher- and child-initiated learning.

The framework also places emphasis on writing a wide range of texts in a variety of forms and media. Multi-modal texts are specifically included and there is explicit reference to the use of ICT. Chapter 6 explores this range and illustrates how creating a diversity of texts can inspire young writers and deepen their understanding of the extraordinary power of the written word.

But although we recognise the importance of the renewed framework for teachers in English primary schools and welcome many of its changes in emphasis, we seek to do more than just show you how you might put it into practice – you will receive plenty of advice about that from other quarters. The iceberg model which we have outlined in this chapter indicates the potential for thinking even more deeply and perhaps more imaginatively. Our central ambition is to help you build a culture of writing in your school: a culture in which everyone loves writing; making it and reading it. When you walk into that school the power and delight of writing is everywhere: published on the walls; published in the books we have made together; published and celebrated through all sorts of technology; celebrated in the excited talk of teachers and children; read aloud for friends, family and community. And everyone who works and learns to write in that school is very lucky.

2 | Getting out more

'Where do you get your ideas from?' Writers are often asked this question, which seems to suggest that if only we go to the same place as they did, we will find a story too. But stories rarely come from one place. Usually, they have been pieced together using ideas gathered over time from various people and settings. Writers write from their own experiences having collected as many details as they can along the way. They search out new ideas in books, pictures, television programmes, games and music but most importantly, from stepping outside their front door.

That is why it is essential that children get the opportunity to explore what is beyond the four walls of their classroom. Good Foundation Stage practitioners understand the value of linking learning to the outside world. A Foundation Stage classroom keeps its doors wide open so that children can sense and experiment and learn. There is a shared belief that there is 'no such thing as bad weather, only the wrong clothing' and because of this, many classrooms store clothes that will suit the sun, the rain and the chill. They take the time to stamp in puddles and to feel the heavy thud of rain on their heads. There is a clear and deliberate connection between the outside world and the classroom, linking learning with reality and giving it purpose. And the children in these classrooms talk excitedly about these experiences. Such practice should not be confined to the Foundation Stage.

Recently, we asked some Year 4 children to look at a picture of grass and find words to describe it. There were various responses, 'green . . . fresh . . . soft' and so on. Then we went outside and played on it, touched it, got up close to it. It is not surprising that the responses were quite different, 'spotted with dew . . . like silky hair . . . soft like a cushion . . . patchy . . . tickly . . . feathery fingers'. When children work outdoors they take greater risks with language because they want to talk clearly about the new things they have discovered. There is a sense of wonder from working outside that cannot be matched in a classroom. It makes children want to voice their excitement.

The activities and processes outlined in this chapter can be used in the outdoor spaces of your school grounds or on school trips. They can be adapted to suit all the primary phases and all levels of ability. Most of all, they are fun and easy to manage.

Starter activities for working outdoors

Children often associate going outdoors with 'playtime' and therefore, a sense of freedom. This is a very positive energy, which, if cleverly channelled, can lead to lively, interesting writing. Whenever we venture outdoors with a new class we introduce games and structures that help them to tune into the world around them as well as getting used to working in a larger space. We aim to awaken the senses, excite the imagination, encourage children to think and talk and then to write.

Starter activity: Objects and experts

Before you even take the children outdoors, it is a good idea to teach them how to examine fine details. Moving straight into a large outdoor space and being asked to observe things can be quite a challenge – the senses are so bombarded that it is difficult to know where to start.

This activity brings objects from nature into the classroom and helps children to find the language to describe them.

Resources

- Paper bags or boxes – at least enough for one between two children.
- Self-adhesive notes.
- A selection of natural objects according to the season (e.g. autumn leaves, petals, etc.), again enough for one between two children.

Steps for this activity

- Put the objects you have chosen inside paper bags and give them out to the children. They should not be able to see the object at all.
- Explain that they will be given one minute only to notice as much as they can about the object inside the bag. Encourage them to use all their senses as much as possible.
- After one minute, ask the children to return the items to the bag.
- Give the children a further three minutes to write as many questions as they can think of about the object. They should write one question per self-adhesive note and stick them on the desk or the paper bag.
- Ask the children, still in pairs, to give each other a number 1 or 2. To begin with, number ones are 'the experts', number twos the questioners. Within these roles, number ones do their best to think of answers to the questions. Stress that the

children don't have to know the real answers – what they don't know they make up. After a minute or so, ask them to swap roles.

Although the children might not know the exact answers to the questions, they start to think of interesting responses and because it is only a game, they don't need to worry about right or wrong answers. This activity really encourages children to take something small and scrutinise it so deeply that they are looking beneath the surface.

Starter activity: Make me a . . .

This game teaches children to think and move sensibly and creatively within a space. It requires them to use their imagination and work as a team.

Resources

A space large enough for children to stand in a circle.

Starting point

- Ask the children to stand in a space.
- Begin working as a whole class. Explain to the children that they are going to be given instructions, but the challenge is to carry them out without any talking at all.
- Giving them about a minute to complete each shape ask them to . . .
    make me a circle,
    make me a rectangle,
    make me a straight line.

Development

- Now the children are in a straight line, tell them that they have to move from the classroom to the outdoors following the steps of the person in front; still with no talking at all.
- Once outdoors, ask them to move into groups. The rule still applies – instructions should only be carried out through gesture, not through talk.
- Ask them to make the following using only their bodies (suggestions will be adapted according to the age of the children):
    make me a full stop,
    make me a comma,
    make me an exclamation mark.
- Finally, introduce images or settings related to texts you are studying in class . . .
    make me a dagger,

make me a crown (if you are working on Macbeth),
make me a teddy bear's picnic (if you are working on Goldilocks).

After children have played this game, praise the way they have moved around the space in such a controlled and sensible way. Point out how cleverly they used their imaginations and how effectively they functioned as a group. If you need to refocus them when working outside, you can quickly return to this game. Asking them to do something like make a whole-class exclamation mark will draw them back together as a group.

Starter activity: The noticing game

This teaches essential skills that real writers use. It encourages children to be much keener observers who pick up on the sorts of subtleties that make writing interesting.

Resources

An outdoor space with plenty to look at, big enough for children to walk around in.

Starting point

- Once children have found a space to stand in, ask them to close their eyes.
- While their eyes are still closed, ask them to point to a feature in the space – a bench, for example, or perhaps a litter bin.
- The children open their eyes and see how close their estimation is.
- Ask the children to move around the space again and as they do, suggest that they should notice as many things as they can, then ask them to stop and close their eyes.
- Call out a new feature and ask the children to point to it with their eyes still closed.
- After a while, a child can be chosen to take the place of the teacher. They enjoy being great at 'noticing' because they get to catch out their classmates.

Children are often surprised by the initial inaccuracy of their estimations, but they are not discouraged. As they play this light-hearted, non-competitive game, they improve very quickly, noticing smaller and smaller details. They learn how to see rather than just to look.

Outdoor writing activities

It is well worth investing in some clipboards and finding a place in the classroom to store waterproofs and wellies. The first steps of these activities can be used in isolation as enjoyable games that improve children's observational skills. But we also suggest some ways of linking the activities to extended writing.

Writing activity 1: Bringing the outdoors in

This is an effective follow-up to the 'noticing' games because children will have developed a greater sense of awareness of the world around them.

Possible writing outcome: A description of a journey from a fairy-tale or myth, written from the character's point of view.

Resources

- An interesting, fairly confined outdoor space where there are different textures and sounds.
- Clipboards, paper and pencils for jotting.

Starting point

- Ask the children to walk around the area, moving in and out of each other looking for spaces. Keep reminding them to look for space. When the children seem to be evenly scattered, ask them to stop.
- In the space that they are standing in, ask the children to look carefully at the different types of texture they can see in the space. There might be bark chippings, paving slabs, leaves – even a small space can contain quite varied textures. Ask the children to jot down three different textures they have noticed. Challenge them to be as descriptive as possible. Encourage them to touch things with their fingers and feel things under their feet. They should try to find words to describe their experience as clearly as possible and there should be contrasts between each texture. Ask them to use words that say what they really see, rather than the sorts of words they might use every day. For example, a Year 3 child we worked with wrote 'scratchy bark, slimy leaves, delicate grass'.
- Ask them to move to another space. This time, they should jot down three sounds they can hear. Make sure they have plenty of time to listen and ask them to think about where the sounds are coming from.
- Finally, in a different space, they should jot down three different things they can see. They should not just write down names, they need to be as expressive as they can so that the reader can see exactly what they see.

How this leads to writing – the word carpet

Step one

The class now move indoors. A school hall is ideal for this activity, where words can be spread out carefully and read clearly.

Within the space you are working, mark out key features from the outdoor area, for example, a wall or a hedge, so that children see where to put their words. Now ask children to refer to the jottings they have made. They are going to create the outdoor landscape using words. Use A5-sized paper and big, chunky pens, so the writing can be read easily as they walk around the space. They should record each of their nine words or phrases on separate pieces of paper and map them into the appropriate position in the hall, laying them face up on the floor.

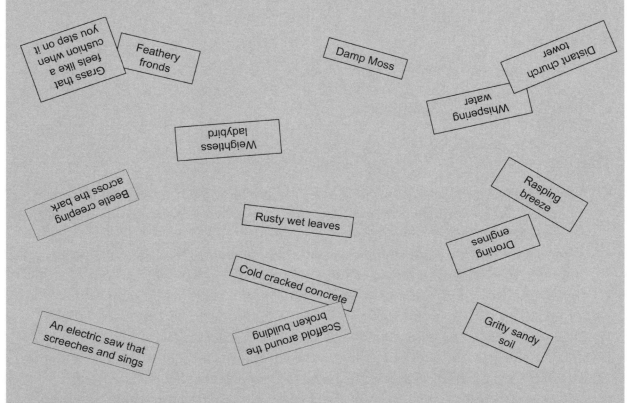

Figure 2.1 The word carpet

Step two

You will now have a carpet of words spread across the floor (see Figure 2.1). You can create an instant soundscape by asking children to walk in and out of the words, calling them out as they read them, for example, 'sweeping branches . . . sweet smelling yellowed leaves . . .'. Encourage the children to notice sounds that flow into one another well, because they might want to use these ideas later on in their writing.

Ask them to listen out for contrasts – 'creaking branches' contains much harder sounds than 'airy earth'. Remind them that writers often use contrasts to heighten tension or create suspense. When you go back to class you can show them poems like 'The Highwayman' that illustrate this point beautifully.

Step three

Now the children have a carpet of descriptive language, they will need to learn how to thread the words together into coherent sentences and paragraphs. The first stage is to encourage them to talk.

Children should now move into pairs and have a number, one or two. Number one is a character from a text you are using, number two is the narrator of the story. Number one has to close their eyes and experience the story, number two has to guide the character through the carpet of words, describing what can be seen and heard. They then swap over. At certain points, the teacher can stop and intervene, calling out prompts . . . 'Suddenly they have stopped very still. Why? What can they hear?'

Step four

Collect up the word carpet and pin it on to a working wall the next day. This will now be a reference for writing.

Show extracts from texts that describe journeys. You will need to decide on the style of writing you want the children to produce: will it be an outdoor chase, or a spooky journey through the night? Analyse the ways in which suspense is created through rhythm and pace. Encourage children to steal words from the texts you are reading, either by highlighting, recording or jotting.

Step five

Model writing a description of a character travelling through a landscape. Pick some of the children's words, add some of your own and use ideas from the texts you have read. Make sure children see you make alterations, crossings out and word improvements. This will give the children more confidence to have a go at writing and improve their own work because they have seen their own teacher undertake this process themselves.

Writing activity 2: Hide, write and seek

Possible writing outcome: To produce an instructional text and/or descriptions of a setting.

Resources

- Objects to hide, e.g. puppets.
- Two 'hiding' areas.
- An extra adult.
- Pens and paper.

Starting point

- Arrange the class into groups of about six, then split each group of six into two groups of three, named A and B. Groups A and B are going to hide puppets from each other.
- Direct all the A groups and the B groups to two separate areas. It is important that As and Bs cannot see each other.

How this leads to writing

Children find a good hiding place for their puppets. When they have done this, their task is to write a detailed description for the other group, to lead them to the hiding place.

It is very important that teachers give children prompts before they start. Ideally, descriptions should be modelled so that children are clearer about expectations.

- The children will need to know where the other group will enter the space.
- They will need to use all their senses in order to make the trail exciting, encouraging the reader to notice as many things as possible.
- They will want to find a way of stopping the other group getting to the end too quickly.

When the descriptions have been completed, they are exchanged between As and Bs and the search for the puppets begins. For example:

> Hear the wind sing through the chimes, leading you to the gravelled path. Follow the path this way and that until knotted willow arches above your head. Twist and dip through the willow tunnel beneath outstretched fingers of light. When the tunnel ends, turn towards the church spire and walk forward until chips of bark soften your steps. Continue until the

trees become more dense and look for the totem pole, hidden by leafy branches. Carefully search its shadows for a secret.

Extending the writing activity

You might want to give children the opportunity to make their descriptions as clear as possible. In some cases, it may be appropriate to mark the work first and allow the children to redraft. If you would rather they went through this process, you could ask them to hide the puppets from children in another class, then having to wait to play the game will not be so much of a problem.

Younger children will enjoy taking digital photographs of the puppet's journey: these can then be printed out, or set up on the computer and sequenced. Children can annotate them with a simple word or phrase. Most important is that in the 'hide', 'write' and 'seek' stages of this game children are looking carefully and noticing details that they might otherwise miss. At the writing stage, they face the challenge of knowing just how much to tease their readers – too much and the reader will lose interest, too little and they will find their object too quickly and enjoy little challenge. Like most writing, you need to think carefully about your reader.

Writing activity 3: Scavenger hunt

Children adore this activity which involves working with a partner or a group on a sort of word treasure hunt. Because there is a sense of discovery, they enjoy collecting interesting language and do their best to be as original as they can.

Possible writing outcome: To create a rhythmic poem.

Resources

- A list of things to hunt for.
- Clipboards.
- Pens or pencils.
- An interesting outdoor space.

Starting point

Children are organised into pairs or small groups. Mixed ability groupings should be encouraged.

Present them with a list of interesting items to search for. For example:

- Something to write with.
- Something that smells nice.
- Something that is nice to touch.
- Something fragile that needs to be handled carefully.
- Something that you can't see.
- Something that makes more than one sound.

How this leads to writing

Rather than asking the children to return with bunches of precious wild flowers, insist that they only return with words. The words must provide a sensory picture of every object they have identified.

Emphasise that you are not simply asking for a list of items. The writing must be as expressive as possible. The language does not have to be complicated, they can choose simple words to describe what they have experienced, but they must explain it as clearly as they can.

Extended writing

The class listens carefully as each group feeds back their responses. If there are extra words and phrases that they like, allow children to record them. For example, a Year 4 group we worked with had:

> Crumbly muddy bark
> Sweet-smelling yellowed leaf
> Wet earth
> Weightless ladybird
> Cold damp air that bites your cheeks
> Chattering, whistling bird

When the rest of the class heard what the group had written they decided they liked 'crumbly' and 'weightless', so they jotted those words down. Another group had used the phrase 'glistening grass', so they decided to add those words to their list.

Tell the children that they are going to piece these words together into a poem. Each verse line will have ten syllables. Model how this might be done, showing how words can be carefully chosen for effects such as alliteration, repetition or personification. The Year 4 group we worked with wrote:

In cold damp air that bites your cheeks, leaves fall
Through wet crumbling earth weightless insects crawl
Sweet-smelling grass glistens in morning light

Children enjoy this activity, especially if the writing can be done while still outdoors. Hearing the sound of the breeze as you write can be very relaxing. When working outdoors in this way, children approach tasks with a kind of gentle reverence, capturing the delicate moments that they have experienced through carefully chosen words.

Writing activity 4: Nightline

Teachers who have been on an outward-bound holiday with their class will probably be familiar with the idea of 'Nightline' which is often used as a team-building exercise, though it can also be a powerful stimulus for writing. In this game, the sense of sight is removed, encouraging childrem to rely entirely on their other senses.

Possible writing outcome: To write a commentary for an action film.

Resources

- A safe outdoor trail with about five key points ready planned.
- Old clothes.
- Blindfolds (optional).
- An extra adult.

Starting point

- Take the children to an area a short distance from where your trail will be. Ask them to stand in a line, one in front of the other.
- Now ask them to put their hand on the shoulder of the person in front of them.
- The child at the front should take hold of a line. The teacher takes the other end and uses this to lead the children through the course.
- Explain to the children that it is important that they keep speaking to each other. The messages the teacher gives at the front of the line need to be relayed all the way to the back.
- Although we have never met a child who has not enjoyed this activity, tell children that they can have a 'safe signal' which you can agree on as a class. This means that if they are uncomfortable with the activity at any point it can instantly be stopped.

Development

- Lead the children towards the trail and tell them when you are starting.
- Make sure you give clear directions and vary how you expect them to move through the course. For example, you may want them to crawl along the grass. Guide the first child carefully down to the floor, and remind the children that they must keep passing the instructions on to each other as they move to the end of the line.
- You may want them to walk over a little bridge – if this is the case, carefully guide their hand on to the rail.

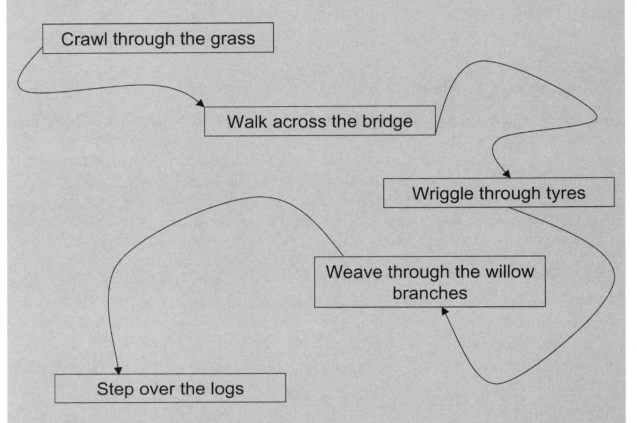

Figure 2.2 An example of a 'Nightline trail'

- An extra adult should be standing back watching the children move along the course, giving further guidance if necessary.
- When the children have completed the trail, ask them to keep their eyes closed/ blindfolds on and guide them to an area away from the trail (this could even be back to your own classroom).

How this leads to writing

Ask the children to create a 'sensory map' of their experience. They must not write down the actual names of things they think they have passed through, but just describe the sensations. They could do this in groups or pairs on large pieces of paper. Also asking them to write a self-adhesive note for each idea works well, because they can move them around and they don't have to worry about running out of space. Afterwards they will be eager to add the names of the places they think they have moved through.

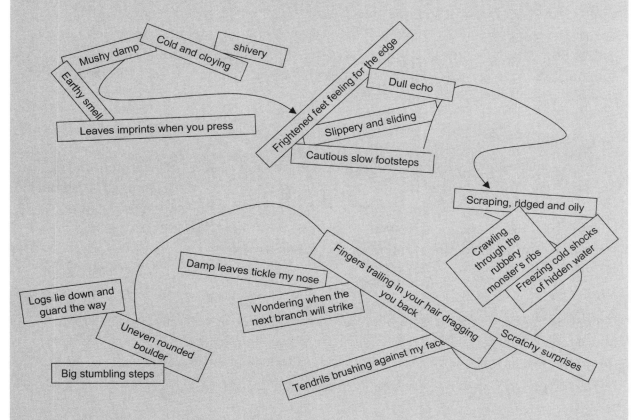

Figure 2.3 A Year 4 sensory map

Carrying the sensory maps with you, return to the trail so that the children can see it. Ask them to move through the trail with their eyes open. They should identify which parts match with their descriptions.

Extending the writing activity

Now you can encourage the children to start piecing together words and ideas into sentences and paragraphs.

Step one

Ask one child from each group to move through the trail, and ask the others to do a live commentary, each taking a different section of the route. Their sensory map provides the notes they need for good language ideas. After they have tried this, discuss the difficulties they experienced, such as how do you keep the ideas flowing? How could the language you used be improved?

Step two

Show the children some text that describes action moving through the outdoors. It could be a description from *Little Red Riding Hood*, or perhaps an extract from *Northern Lights* by Philip Pullman. It could even be an example from a travel diary. Discuss the way it is presented, how word rhythm is manipulated and also highlight some of the language used. Encourage the children to borrow some of the language, ready to use for their own action video.

Step three

Record a video clip of an action adventure – a mountain biking competition that hurtles through trees, or even some motor racing. Show this to the children. Encourage them to listen to the commentary, noticing the phrases used. Ask them to call out phrases they like as they hear them. When they have finished watching the clip, give them a minute to jot down as many good phrases as they remember.

Step four

Model for the class a good example of a prepared script of commentary for an action film. Model it for two steps of the trail, then allow them to work through the process themselves. You will then have the opportunity to look at their work, mark it and reflect on it the next day, ready for the final steps in writing.

When the children have completed the description there are many ways in which it could be presented for an audience. It could provide the voice-over for a film the children actually make of their journey through the trail. It could accompany photographs to go into a brochure format that would advertise the trail to another class or another school. It could even be read out and recorded as a radio clip of a journey through an obstacle course. The children would have tremendous fun producing a 'live' effect.

Working and writing outdoors is not just about observing changes in the seasons or linking writing to work on plants. When we take children outside the classroom we are opening up a world of possibilities that should be frequently explored – every week if possible. The more discoveries children make, the more they will search for language to describe what they have found. And they will learn that if they can write about these discoveries, their experiences can be relived and remembered for a very long time.

3 Good books matter

It may be quite usual to meet avid readers who write very little, but it is very rare to find a good writer who does not read. So a school that gives very high priority to the teaching of writing will also be one where good books are plentiful; where good literature is enjoyed and celebrated; and where everyone in school – children, teaching and non-teaching staff, parents and governors – reads, knows, talks and cares about books. Building this kind of 'reading culture' in a school takes commitment and hard work from everyone, but the benefits for children are immense. Children who are part of a reading culture learn how being truly literate is about so much more than being able to read well enough to make sense of what they need to at secondary school, or to get a job, or to read at a level which allows them to function in the adult world, however important all those things may be. Once welcomed into the world of the reader, children become part of a community which will enrich and sustain them for the rest of their lives. The world of the reader is one with many rich connections and, once guided into it by nurturing and knowledgeable adults, one in which children can find their own places based on their own preferences as one good book leads to another. No one reader can be expected to know their way around the whole of that immense landscape, but if a child is to become a good writer they are likely to begin their exploration early and never stop.

Starting at the beginning

It is often said that parents are a child's first teachers. Teachers know that many children are lucky enough to be born into families where they are given books and read to from only a few weeks old. These children will often start school with a growing love of the written word, wide experience of books, and a developing sense of what they enjoy. Many have begun their journey into the world of the reader well before they begin their formal education. Many, of course, have not. But there are very practical steps that a school can take to reach out into its community and encourage the development of a reading culture from the very first stages.

Recent years have seen an unprecedented growth in the provision of early years education and childcare facilities. Many schools already have very strong links with the settings in their areas and these settings in turn often have very strong relationships with parents. Getting key members of staff from your school to make connections with these settings can be a very powerful way of reaching out to parents before their children start school, forming positive relationships that will endure throughout their education. Once such relationships are established, they can encourage parents to read to and with their children, to share books with them, talking about the stories, the illustrations and the themes of the books and relating them to their own lives and experiences.

Of course it is important to recognise and be sensitive to the fact that not all parents have positive experiences of and attitudes to reading themselves. There will be those for whom school and all that is connected with it has only negative associations. In such circumstances, opening channels of communication early and doing whatever it takes to keep them open becomes more important than ever. And schools can do a great deal to enable the building of relationships between parents and families so that they become mutually supportive: sharing books, reading to and with each others' children, perhaps visiting the local library together.

It can also be very powerful to engage older children in this process of building a reading community from the start. Those with younger siblings will know some of the places where mothers and babies meet. Older children might, for instance, design posters and leaflets that can be displayed and distributed at the local health centre, encouraging parents to read to and share books with their children. Are there local parent and toddler groups? If so, children can also make leaflets and posters for them, thinking carefully about their intended audience. There may, for example, be a number of languages other than English in the community which children speak themselves, or they may have access to those who do speak them and who can help with translation. Perhaps a group of children might organise some fund-raising to buy and maintain a small library of books for babies and toddlers that can be loaned through these groups. Some groups may be very willing to allow older children to visit and read to parents and toddlers – young children often delight in the company of older children, who can provide very powerful early role models. Children might also undertake a project where they research and produce their own books for younger children. These may be carefully structured and illustrated picture story books, or perhaps talking books made using ICT which might either be put on to CDs for younger children, or these children and their parents could be invited into school to see and hear them.

Involving older children in the process of building a reading community is one way in which it can be built from within rather than imposed from outside. The development of such a community is far more likely to be successful if it is done by those who are active members of it, so everyone feels that they are part of it and it is part of them. It is much less likely to find success if people feel they are being told what to do by those who claim to know what's best for them. Talking with and involving as many members of your community as you can is absolutely vital.

Staff who love books too

Building a community of readers in and around a school necessarily requires teachers and other adults who are themselves knowledgeable about and enjoy reading children's literature. Given the immense demands that there are on a teacher's time, this can be very difficult, but its value cannot be overstated. If you are going to guide children into the world of the reader, rather than just teach them to decode text, then you need to know as much of that landscape as possible: where the major landmarks are; where some smaller areas of interest to a particular reader might be; what is new and about to appear on the horizon.

Although there will inevitably be some teachers with more enthusiasm for children's literature than others, knowledge of what is available and good cannot rest with only one member of staff. All schools will have a designated literacy co-ordinator or English subject leader, but their workload is immense involving as it does the detailed analysis of assessment data, planning and leading responses to issues that arise, reporting to school leaders and governors: the list goes on. Expecting them, in addition, to be the sole or main source of knowledge and information about children's literature is asking a great deal. In addition, and to work closely with the literacy co-ordinator/English subject leader, schools might consider designating a member of staff as a kind of 'children's literature champion' – a teacher or perhaps a teaching assistant who has specific responsibility for promoting a reading culture in school and keeping up to date with what is new. They may organise book fairs and other events in school, attend networks organised by the local authority, the library service, or among local clusters of schools. Importantly though, they will become a point of reference within school for both staff and children from whom they can get advice and guidance on what is available and what they might read next.

Spreading that knowledge and enthusiasm among other members of staff is also crucial in building a reading culture. Children's literature updates can be standing items on staff meeting agendas, perhaps setting up a rolling programme whereby members of staff take turns to update everyone on what they and their children have read and enjoyed recently. In-service days (or parts of them) might be given over to building and deepening staff knowledge of the literature that is available in their school and beyond. Each member of staff can be given a small selection of books to read in preparation for the day and asked to lead the rest of the staff in some activities which share, explore and celebrate what has been read. And, of course, all of this needs to be done in a climate of mutual support and celebration: if it is simply imposed or demanded from above it may have an effect which runs entirely counter to that intended. In a genuine reading culture everyone reads because they love to.

Local sources of support

Within the school's immediate community and beyond it there will be a number of organisations, groups and individuals who might help. We are lucky enough to work in a local authority that has an excellent schools' library service. As well as loaning books to schools, they have staff with unrivalled knowledge of children's literature, particularly the thousands of new books that are published each year. They offer services to individual schools, including auditing the school library, removing outdated stock and advising on new book buying. They also organise events such as book quizzes and the shadowing of awards for children's literature. It is well worth investing time to find out what services are available in your area.

The networks provided through local authority advisory services also vary considerably. Some may offer access to networks and other meetings where you can keep up to date with what is new and exchange ideas for good books and ways of working with them. A good deal of support is also currently offered through the Primary Strategy. You may also have networks available more locally and, if not, you could look into establishing one through which interested teachers and others can meet to update each other and share ideas.

You may also be surprised by what other sources of support there are in your local community. Across the country, significant numbers of adults are members of book groups and circles; these may well be worth contacting to see if there are possibilities for establishing a sub- or spin-off group for those (not only teachers) who are interested in children's literature. It's also well worth asking around to find out if there are local writers in your area – they may write for magazines and other journals, even the parish magazine, but they are potential sources of support as you build a culture of reading and writing in the school.

Keeping up to date

In addition to what may be available locally, there are plenty of national organisations and journals which can help you keep up to date with what is new and good in children's literature. Possibilities include:

- Subscription to a magazine like *Books for Keeps* which includes articles about children's books and a regular review section with star ratings for new titles.
- Membership of organisations like the United Kingdom Literacy Association (UKLA) which not only publish regular newsletters and journals, but also organise courses and conferences.
- Membership of the National Centre for Language and Literacy, based at the University of Reading, who produce excellent publications and also offer courses and conferences.
- The Centre for Literacy in Primary Education (CLPE) offers a range of support, and teachers will find their publication *Core Books*, which is updated every two years, particularly useful when reviewing and updating their provision of books.
- Membership of the National Association for the Teaching of English (NATE) which offers a very good range of support nationally and locally.

- Keeping up to date with book awards like the Carnegie Medal and the Kate Greenaway Medal, or the Smarties Prize – the long- and shortlists for these prizes give a terrific insight into the best of new children's books

Only the best will do

With several thousand new titles published every year, no one school can expect to buy everything that is available, nor would they want to. The abundance of children's books from which to choose is something to be celebrated, but all teachers know that their financial resources are always limited and that their money needs to be spent carefully and wisely. Necessarily this means making judgements about quality: some books are very much better than others and there can be no excuses for wasting money on books that are tacky, trivial or patronising, however cheap they might be. Schools with a rich and well-developed reading culture have a clear book-buying policy, agreed with children, staff, governors and parents. Every title they purchase must meet their own high expectations and be good enough to put before the young readers in their community.

Making such judgements about the quality of books in your school does not mean that you cannot be inclusive and open to a wide range of literature. Good readers have a very varied diet that will include fiction and non-fiction, newspapers, magazines and journals, books that are bought to be read once and those to be kept and treasured. This variety needs to be reflected in what you have and encourage in school: many children will want to bring in magazines and comics that reflect their particular interests, or spin-offs from films or a favourite television series. It can all form part of a rich and varied reading diet. Although the examples we give later are predominantly fiction, we should also stress the importance of a range of high-quality, up-to-date non-fiction. Not only will this support work across the rest of the taught curriculum, it will also include a range of books that children can 'dip into' and browse. The selection will build over time to reflect a wide range of children's interests from football or riding to fishing and dancing. Include, encourage and celebrate all that you can.

The school as a community of readers

All that we have mentioned so far, from supporting new parents to contacting readers and writers in your local community, has a huge contribution to make in laying the foundations for a school community which loves and values good books. But there is also a need to develop and sustain that community in school; to help children become aware of good books and the connections between them; and to celebrate the delight of reading.

As we have already stressed, reading aloud to children should be a regular and valued part of life in any primary school. If children are read to every day, they develop and sustain an awareness and interest in the written word, gain an appreciation of what it means to read and write well, and accept literature as a natural and pleasurable part of their lives. Good teachers take this responsibility seriously, taking time over the careful selection of appropriate books and deliberately developing their ability to read aloud.

There are also a number of very effective games and other strategies which encourage children to think critically and talk together about what they have read and enjoyed.

Book bingo

This game is best played after a weekend or holiday when everyone has read a new book. They have the book with them when they walk around the space. On a given signal from the teacher, children stop, then form pairs and talk about the books they have read. As soon as they find a connection between their two books, they call 'bingo!' and the rest of the class stop talking and hear what their connection is – it may be to do with the theme, the author, the illustrator, the setting, the plot, or the characters. Other children and the teacher then have the chance to comment and maybe add in some connections of their own before the children walk again and are given the signal to find a new partner with whom to share their book.

The book web

This game is played with the children seated in a circle. You will also need a ball of string. One child is chosen to start the web: they have the ball of string and hold it while they talk about a book they have just read. As soon as another child sees a connection with something they have read, they raise a hand and are asked to say what the connection is. Keeping hold of the end of the string, the first child rolls the ball to the child who has made a connection – that child then talks about their book until another sees a connection with theirs. Each time the ball of string is passed on, the child who made the last connection keeps hold of it before rolling the rest of the ball on to the next. As the game develops, the class make a huge web of connections between all that they have read. You can finish the game by seeing if you can stand up and move around while keeping the web intact.

Similar 'webs of connection' can be created as displays on the wall, each child making their own version of a cover for their book and then using string or wool to show the connections between them all.

There's a book over there that . . .

For this game you will need a reasonably large space and plenty of books to choose from – ideally more books than there are children in the class. Spread the books out, either on the floor or on tables around the room. Divide the children into groups of about four. When you ask them to, the children walk among the books, noticing what they can, but not touching the books at this stage. On a given signal from you, each child moves to a book and has a minute to notice and remember as much about it as possible; looking at the cover, the blurb and anything else they can in the time available. When the minute is over, the children return to their groups and each has a timed slot of 15–30 seconds to feed back as much about their book as they can. Then you signal for them to walk among the books again. Next time you ask them to stop and choose a book, their decision may be informed either by what has taken their attention as they walk, or by something they heard in their group. This game should be very fast-paced, quickly building impressions of what is on offer and helping children to make informed choices.

Good books and the young writer

The connections between what young writers write and what they read are many and complex. Since the introduction of the National Literacy Strategy in 1998, the practice of taking books and extracts as models for children's writing has become much more widespread. This may be at the whole text level; for example, taking one of Ted Hughes's creation stories, exploring how it is structured and using this structure as a basis for children to write their own. Children and teachers will also look at the level of the sentence to see how a particular writer constructs and combines sentences to achieve a particular effect. These approaches may have echoes of Philip Pullman's advice to young writers to 'read like a butterfly and write like a bee', but it is important that he is talking about much more than mere mimicry. The more widely young writers read, the greater the stock of stories they have, and the greater the richness and diversity of language they have experienced and upon which they can draw for their own writing.

As we also pointed out in Chapter 1, good books have in themselves the power to transport their readers and give them imagined experiences that they could not otherwise have. *Treasure Island* is a tale full of quite alarming dangers, but the young reader can curl up in a chair or lie on the beach and be taken to those other times and places in perfect safety. And to do so he just needs to *read* the book. Analysing its structure, unpicking its sentences and spotting the author's use of adjectives, reviewing it and designing a cover for it may all have their place, but the sheer delight of reading it for its own sake and trusting the effect that it will have on a young writer is vital.

Recommended reads

As we have emphasised throughout, the range of good books available for children is quite dazzling. It would be well beyond our scope here to make particular recommendations, still less to provide an exhaustive list – we have suggested other sources for such help. What follows is just a tiny selection of ten books that we have used extensively in the classroom and which we have seen have an impact on what and how children write. You and your classes will, of course, have favourites of your own, but we have chosen these to give a small taste of what we have found to be good.

Owl Babies, Martin Waddell, illustrated by Patrick Benson
Walker Books ISBN 0-7445-3167-5

What is it about?

This is a real favourite with younger children. It tells of three baby owls who wake up one night to find that their mother has gone. Very simply, the author tells of their distress and anxiety and how they comfort and support each other until their mother returns. It is beautifully illustrated so as to give the reader wonderful insight into how the characters are thinking and feeling.

What is so good about it?

Much of the story's strength lies in its delightful simplicity. We are told how at the beginning the baby owls live happily with their mother. Their stable and comfortable home life is disturbed briefly when she disappears, but all is well by the end when she returns home again. In the tradition of such animal stories, all the baby owls have recognisable human traits with which children can identify and its themes are familiar to most: the fear of being left alone; seniority and solidarity among siblings when faced with a crisis. And ultimately, it is completely reassuring.

What can they do and write?

Thoughtful questioning and discussion about the owls and their predicament can illicit all sorts of responses from children. It may well result in them talking about times they have been left alone and/or have been afraid, though such discussion will clearly need careful handling. Some of these experiences might be written about, or the children might devise their own versions of the story by inventing new characters. It is also quite easy to get hold of puppets of the owls and their mother, encouraging children to play with retelling and extending the story in their own ways.

Click, Clack, Moo: Cows That Type, Doreen Cronin, pictures by Betsy Lewin
Pocket Books ISBN 0-743-46151-7

What is it about?

This is a fable about the power of writing. Farmer Brown's cows find a typewriter in their barn and learn how to use it. Once able to write, they use their typewriter to demand better conditions for themselves and the hens, withdrawing milk and egg production until their conditions are met. Farmer Brown eventually gives in to their demands in return for which they give up their typewriter – but only to pass it on to the ducks who in turn start making their own demands.

What is so good about it?

The idea of cows learning to type is funny and playful, but the story also holds an important truth: writing is a very powerful medium and it can be used to change things for the better.

What can they do and write?

This is a really good story to dramatise with children, getting them up and actively retelling the story through sound and movement. When the story reaches the point where Duck goes to see the cows on Farmer Brown's behalf, the teacher can take the role of Duck while the children are the cows. Presented with Farmer Brown's letter and its demands, the cows discuss what they want to do next – their reply must be carefully written on the typewriter. Once they decide what to do, their story often departs from Doreen Cronin's original and all sorts of possibilities open up. It's great if you can get hold of an old typewriter for children to experiment with and this can often help reluctant writers by offering them another medium.

Dogger, Shirley Hughes
Picture Lions ISBN 0-00-661464-7

What is it about?

This is the story of Dave and his toy Dogger who gets lost on the afternoon before the School Summer Fair. Dogger eventually turns up on the toy stall at the fair, but is bought by another little girl before Dave can find the necessary money to buy him back himself. It is Dave's big sister Bella who eventually saves Dogger by giving up the brand new teddy she has just won in the raffle.

What is so good about it?

This is an example of beautifully skilled storytelling. It has a simple domestic setting which will be familiar to lots of children even though the book is now three decades old. Dave is skilfully placed as the middle child between his older sister who acquires as many soft toys as possible and his younger brother who just chews things. Dave likes only Dogger, so the horror of losing him is absolute. Shirley Hughes's skill as a storyteller gives the reader an almost perfectly constructed plot: just when things seem hopeless, she offers hope; just when things look to be on the point of being resolved, she makes her reader work a little harder.

What can they do and write?

There are lots of elements of this story which you can explore with children. Any of the characters can be 'hot-seated' to explore different perspectives on the events. It can be particularly effective to get a Dogger puppet and talk to him to explore what happened to him while he was lost – this might lead up to telling the story from Dogger's point of view.

It is also a very good story to retell with children, getting them to act out different parts of it as the teacher narrates. This can be a very good way of exploring alternative endings. How would the reader feel if Dogger was quite lost and Dave never found him again? What if he had simply turned up in Bella's toy box that first evening? How much does it matter that Dave does not have enough money with him when he first finds Dogger on the toy stall? All these questions help children to explore why the plotting of this story is so skilful and so effective.

They might also use the story as a basis for writing 'lost toy' stories of their own. A good way of doing this can be to get children to work in groups and present their story in six pictures which they make using a digital camera. These pictures in effect become their plan for their story, and getting out and about to create them can make the whole business of thinking the plot through much more engaging and enjoyable.

Two Frogs, Chris Wormell
Red Fox ISBN 0-09-943862-3

What is it about?

This is the story of two frogs sitting on a lily pad in the middle of their lake. One of them has a stick which, he explains to the other, will be needed should they be attacked by a dog that swims out to them. While they discuss the improbability of all this, they are attacked, first by a pike, and then by a heron. As things turn out, the stick does save them, but not in the way either might have imagined.

What is so good about it?

This book is very funny and playful. The frogs argue in just the way that children do when one has proposed something very unlikely but insists on defending that proposition to the last. The author unfolds his story very skilfully with plenty of unexpected twists and turns. The illustrations combine with the text to make the hapless frogs and their situation entirely believable.

What can they do and write?

Before you have read any of the text to or with the children, you can just show them one of the illustrations and get them to improvise what they think the conversation between the frogs might be. Apply some tight constraints – perhaps only five lines each – and then get them to write down their dialogue.

Still starting from speaking and listening, conversations can be developed between all sorts of other characters from the story. If the two pike get to chat about what happened, what advice might they give each other? Is there anything a pike should always carry rather than a stick? What about a heron? Have the other frogs in the pond learned anything from the two frogs' experience? What thoughts go through the dog's mind as he lies in his bed waiting for the time for his walk?

In the very playful spirit of the story, several possibilities arise for other texts in a variety of forms. What about a problem page from *Pike Monthly's* (and adverts for a range of related products)? Can they write *A Heron's Guide to Frogging* or perhaps *Self-Defence for Frogs*?

The Jolly Postman or Other People's Letters, Janet and Allan Ahlberg
Heinemann ISBN 0-434-92515-2

What is it about?

This is the story of the Jolly Postman's round delivering letters through a land that is populated by characters from nursery rhymes and traditional stories. Some of the pages are in the form of envelopes and the letters have to be taken out and read separately. The letters weave their way into the stories so, for instance, there is a letter of apology from Goldilocks to the Three Bears, and a solicitor's letter to the Big Bad Wolf sent on behalf of Red Riding Hood.

What is so good about it?

This well-known book is one of extraordinary ingenuity. Having alternate pages in the form of the envelopes which the postman delivers gives each piece of mail a life of its own. The book's style and appearance often lead to the assumption that it is only suitable for younger readers, but the letters, with their variety of text type and complexity, make this book very enjoyable for readers and writers of all ages.

What can they do and write?

Children's understanding of the letters and their contexts can be deepened by creating short scenes depicting how and where they were written and how they are treated on arrival. In the 'arrival scenes' the teacher can take the role of the Jolly Postman and engage in conversation with the recipients about the letters and their contents.

In the story the Jolly Postman only delivers six letters. As emphasised by Janet Ahlberg's illustrations, his round is in a land where all the characters are from traditional stories or nursery rhymes. It is not difficult to generate a list of other characters who might also be on the round. When you have generated a list, assign characters to groups/pairs. Next, you need to generate a list of all the types of writing that can arrive through the post. Alternatively, you could prepare for the project by conducting a survey of post received in children's homes on any one day (or perhaps over a few days).

To decide who should write to whom you need to make a version of the 'story wheel'. Cut two circles of card, one smaller than the other and join them at the centre so that they can turn in relation to each other. Divide both circles into the same number of segments as you have groups/pairs. You then need to write each character on to *both* circles. Once all the segments are full, it's time to 'spin the wheel'. Each character should line up with another – the characters on the outer circle write to those with whom they line up on the inner circle. By doing this you ensure that each group/pair both writes and receives a letter.

Each group/pair can also take responsibility for making a 'house front' for their character based on what they know of the story. The house fronts can include letterboxes, doorbells, etc.

The teacher can take the role of the Jolly Postman and collect and deliver the letters. As he arrives at each house, he engages in conversation about the letter and its contents. This kind of role play is an excellent way of encouraging children to reflect on the wider context into which their writing fits. It also opens up the possibility of developing the project into a performance.

The Silver Swan, Michael Morpurgo, illustrated by Christian Birmingham

Picture Corgi ISBN 0-552-54614-3

What is it about?

Told in the first person, this is the story of a swan coming to an isolated loch. The boy who tells the story becomes fascinated by the swan, watching and feeding her daily. Then a cob arrives and the pair of swans set about nest building, their progress observed by the boy in every detail until the arrival of five cygnets. Then winter makes a late and unwelcome return and when the loch freezes a fox takes her chance to get a meal for her starving cubs. The author turns the consequent events into a very moving story of love and devotion.

What is so good about it?

Wonderfully observed, beautifully written and illustrated, this story captures the absorption into the natural world that comes through the careful observation and particular identification with one living creature. The experience will be familiar to plenty of children whether they live in the city, town or countryside. It's also a fine example of a story built on first-hand experience and detailed observation of the landscape it describes.

What can they do and write?

There are lots of possibilities for using drama techniques to explore the boy's responses at various stages in the story. You might begin by making an image of him watching the arrival of the swan, adding sound and thought-tracking. There are several points in the story at which he might be hot-seated – what did he see? What did he think? Why is he so fascinated by the swan?

Children can experiment with transforming some of the text into poetry, both with passages about the swans and the foxes. Children's ideas about the foxes could also be used to develop a story in which the boy becomes preoccupied with their predicament rather than the swans – how might his views and feelings be different?

The Christmas Miracle of Jonathan Toomey, Susan Wojciechowski, illustrated by P. J. Lynch
Walker Books ISBN 0-7445-5402-0

What is it about?

This is the story of a lonely woodcarver whose wife and child have died some years before the story begins. One day the widow McDowell and her son call at the woodcarver's house and ask him to carve a set of Christmas figures for them. Although he only agrees reluctantly, it is through the carving of the figures and his resultant relationship with the boy and his mother that he can come to terms with his loss.

What is so good about it?

The story is rich in its use of symbol and metaphor to trace the woodcarver's slow recovery from his terrible grief. The characters are beautifully brought to life through a subtle combination of the author's skilfully crafted dialogue and the quite stunning illustrations.

What can they do and write?

There are a number of themes and elements which recur through the story and it is well worth drawing children's attention to how they progress. The knock at the door, the carving of each figure, the sound of the church bells and Jonathan's reaction to them, the food the widow brings with her each time they visit: all are developed subtly as the story unfolds. The knocks at the door, for example, can be brought to life through making a sequence of tableaux or still images. Children can also explore why Jonathan insists on keeping the drawer closed and find ways of dramatising the memories that escape when it is opened.

There are also plenty of opportunities for writing around the story. Each of the character's experiences of the story can be explored by writing their diaries. The sequel to the story also has plenty of possibilities – what becomes of the three characters after that magical Christmas?

The Mousehole Cat, Antonia Barber and Nicola Bayley
Walker Books ISBN 0-7445-2353-2

What is it about?

This is a retelling of a Cornish story about a winter when a great storm comes and stops the people of Mousehole from going to sea to fish. When it looks as if the village will go hungry at Christmas, an old fisherman called Tom and his cat Mowzer decide to brave the storm even though they are risking their lives. It is Mowzer who is able to calm the Great Storm-Cat so that they can take back fish for the rest of the village.

What is so good about it?

The story is told in subtly poetic language based on the local dialect. It captures the total dependence of the community on the sea and what they can take from it. That complex and volatile relationship is beautifully embodied in Mowzer's gentle and respectful calming of the mythic Great Storm-Cat.

What can they do and write?

You can begin the exploration of this story by creating still and moving images of daily life in the village, first as the people, then as the cats that live there. You can experiment with a soundscape to represent the storm and then get pairs of children to improvise the villagers' conversations above the sound of wind and waves. These conversations can then be written down and included in a variety of retellings of events by other villagers. You can also create a circle of lights to represent the harbour, with each child holding a small torch and speaking out their message of hope to the fishing boats. There is also much to explore about the ways in which the story is remembered, by both cats and people.

Quetta, Gary Crew, illustrated by Bruce Whatley
Lothian ISBN 0-7344-0240-6

What is it about?

This story is based on the true events of a court case in which the custody of a three-year-old girl is contested between Mutassa Clark, a young man of nineteen, and Captain Brown and his wife who are in their sixties. Mutassa Clark rescued the girl after the steamship *Quetta* sank in the Torres Strait in 1890. The ship struck a rock and took only three minutes to go down. As Mutassa gives his testimony to the court, Bruce Whatley's dramatic illustrations bring the terrible events of the night to life.

What is so good about it?

This story raises some very important themes about parenthood, race and gender. The rights and wrongs of the case and its outcome continue to interest and engage children and are very relevant today. The real events are skilfully woven into the story and the illustrations make a sharp contrast between vivid first-hand memory and the more distant formality of the courtroom.

What can they do and write?

This is another good story to dramatise. The text can readily be translated into a script. While some children take the roles in the courtroom and bring the proceedings to life, others can enact the events that are described, contrasting the ordered formality of giving testimony with the chaotic terror of the sinking. This can lead to writing and providing further testimony from other passengers.

While the court proceedings take place, the child is 'playing in the yard under the supervision of a constable'. When the judge reaches his decision, Mutassa asks to be allowed to see her. In pairs, children can improvise and explore the scene between the two and use this to inform subsequent writing.

Clockwork or All Wound Up, Philip Pullman
Doubleday ISBN 0-385-40755-6

What is it about?

This is the story of two young craftsmen in a little German town, one a clockmaker and the other a storyteller. Both have failed to complete important pieces of work, and when the central character from the storyteller's unfinished tale unexpectedly walks into the inn where he is reading it, events take a quite chilling turn as story and reality become entangled.

What is so good about it?

Brilliantly written by a master storyteller, this is a tale about the responsibilities that go with the art and craft of storytelling. By paralleling the skills of storytelling with the craft of clockwork making, Philip Pullman illustrates the subtlety and complexity of a well-crafted plot. It is a dark tale with elements of Faust and Frankenstein, but one which older children will enjoy enormously. As the story unfolds, the author adds intriguing comments on his own narrative in boxes that sit within the body of the text.

What can they do and write?

This story almost demands to be read aloud and, particularly when you are reading Fritz's story, it can be greatly enhanced by rearranging the room and perhaps lighting it differently to create the atmosphere of the inn on that winter's evening. It is full of good places to stop, explore and discuss what has happened, and wonder – and write – what might happen next.

Children will also enjoy creating the 'Great Clock of Glockenheim' by using themselves to represent the clockwork figures and carefully animating the movement of the clock. You can also use the idea that the figures come to life when Karl the apprentice brings his figure to join them – what might they have to say to him? And there are so many other parts of this deliciously complex story to lift off the page and dramatise, each offering plenty of opportunities to explore and write elements of it from a variety of viewpoints.

As we have already stressed, this selection of books is not intended to be comprehensive or representative, rather to give a small taste of some of the books we use and the ways in which we use them. There are, of course, very many more to choose from, each with all sorts of possibilities for encouraging, challenging and inspiring children to write. It is worth noticing, however, that we include a number of picture books suitable for older readers – there is no reason why such beautiful books should be overlooked just because children have reached a certain age or stage. Many of them also offer models of writing at a length to which children in the primary school might realistically aspire. None of this should take away the importance or sheer joy of children reading novels of much greater length. Good books matter: all of them.

Using drama and imaginative play

Pretending to be someone or something other than themselves comes very naturally to most children. A child may, for instance, decide quite spontaneously that she is going to be a dog: she scampers around on all fours, barks and whines when she wants something, asks to be taken for a walk, and even expects her food to be given to her on the floor. Quite understandably, parents and other adults place limits on how far they are prepared to join in the game, but lucky children encounter those who understand just how important such behaviour is. Whether he is being a dog or a builder or a dad or a mum, the child engaged in this kind of play creates a world, enters into it, and actively explores the consequences of being there. It demands a sustained effort of imagination: the kind of imagination that is fundamental to becoming a writer.

Some adults tend to associate these playful behaviours solely with early childhood and consequently think of them as something that we 'grow out of': some may even actively discourage it as children grow older. Yet it is that very capacity to suspend the normal rules of time, place and identity and believe together in the worlds we have created that is the basis of theatre, of film, and of the television soap. We all know that the characters that populate *East Enders* or *Coronation Street* are not real, but we still enjoy putting that knowledge on hold for half an hour while we watch them interact with each other and absorb ourselves in the unfolding stories. And *story* is a vital word; for whether it is a child or group of children playing in the role-play area, or a company of actors on the stage of a theatre, their words and their actions usually combine to tell a story. The children in their role-play area are active agents in the making and living of those stories, combining thoughts and feelings, words and actions. Though we don't wish to underestimate its importance and value in the lives of many children, watching film and television is passive in comparison. Those capacities to create worlds and to live in them together, which children often exhibit so spontaneously in the early years, need to be kept alive throughout primary education – and well beyond it – if the imagination that gives rise to them is to be nurtured and developed in young writers. Drama and imaginative play are vital elements of the primary curriculum in their own right, but they can also make a powerful contribution to the development of writers in a number of important ways.

Living an imagined experience

We wouldn't normally allow young children to practise as doctors or car mechanics, but the worlds they create through their role play allow them to do just that. And those same capacities that allow them to be doctors or mechanics allow them to create and live in all sorts of other worlds from a home to a shop to an enchanted forest, even to an undiscovered planet. As children get older, we may use the structures and strategies of drama to create and shape these stories with them, but what they have in common with those early years experiences is that the story is lived out and what happens in it happens because of what we say, do and decide. The more of these stories we make together, the greater the fund of lived stories we have to draw upon when writing.

The mind–body connection

Drama is a very physical discipline: we think and respond through and with our bodies and our voices. For many children this can be a very liberating way of experiencing a story because they bring their whole selves to it. Many schools are now familiar with the notion of 'kinaesthetic learning' or learning through and with the body: learning in this way is at the heart of drama.

Feeling feelings

Feelings live in the body: this is why we experience things like a knot in the stomach or a shortness of breath if we are nervous, or why we might jump up and down when we are happy. We often ask children to talk about feelings, perhaps by asking them how a character in a story might be feeling, only to be disappointed that their responses go little further than 'happy' or 'sad'. But feelings are difficult for anyone, let alone a young child, to talk about in the abstract. We need to experience and *live* them before we can be expected to talk and write about them. An apparently simple game like *blink murder* can help us physically to feel tension, notice its effects, and use those to inform our writing. When children are engaged in longer dramas, they often talk afterwards about how real it *felt*.

Structuring narrative

The ways in which we structure narrative in drama teach us a great deal about how we structure narrative in writing. We often begin dramas by establishing a narrative equilibrium: how things are at the beginning of our story. With younger children, this may involve 'free playing' and 'freezing' as animals in a wood; with older children we might make images of everyday life in a Saxon village. That equilibrium is disturbed by some event: unwelcome visitors to the wood who cut down the trees; or news that neighbouring villages have been raided by Vikings. The tension created by that disturbance will build to a climax or high point of the story: the animals going by night to disable the machines; the villagers successfully defending their homes. And the story will then resolve itself: the animals are left alone to live in their wood; the Saxons make a treaty with their Viking neighbours. Experiencing drama that is structured in this way, and having the connection with written stories made explicit, can help children to a deeper understanding of how writers structure narrative and the effect this might have on their readers

Playing with alternatives

Through drama we can readily explore alternatives in the ways narratives develop. For example, we might ask groups to develop short scenes that show an ending for *Little Red Riding Hood*, view them and discuss the impact of each before children commit to writing an ending of their own. Through drama, those alternatives can be shown and talked about quickly and easily, helping children to approach writing them with greater confidence and certainty.

Putting writing in context

Dramatised stories can often be taken forward by the arrival of a letter, the discovery of a fragment of text, a diary entry or a message. What is important here is that the writing appears in a meaningful social context. In an early years role-play area that has been set up as a health centre, a child might make some marks on a piece of paper and put it on the wall to tell visitors the times at which the surgery is open. What matters is that the child writes and displays her writing for a purpose that is very real in the context of the role play. If she believes in her role as the doctor, the nurse or the receptionist, the writing is tackled readily and confidently and its purpose clearly understood.

Writing to change the story

Click, Clack, Moo, one of the stories we explored in Chapter 3, is a very good example of this. The cows can only communicate by writing and that is how they get things done. When children have taken on the roles of the cows and made decisions about what to write and to whom, they get to see how that writing then changes the developing story. Dramas can often offer opportunities where writing is the only way of changing things – a cruel and tyrannical king may not be willing to see us, but he will accept a letter or petition from us. If children have committed to the drama and believe in the story that is unfolding, they will take great care over drafting such a letter because it has the possibility of changing things for the better.

Using rich language

Children will often use more complex and rich language in their drama and play than they would otherwise. This may be because the roles they have taken on, for example, as police officers or travel agents, need to use specialised language as part of their jobs: early years practitioners are often surprised and delighted by the sophisticated and complex language which children will use in their role play. Or it may be that the experience of the drama has led children to use rich and complex language to describe what they have seen or heard, for example, when they have just enacted being part of the team that went with Howard Carter into the tomb of Tutankhamun. It is important to stress though that this language needs to be captured (by them, by you, or perhaps by a teaching assistant) *as it happens* so that it can be used in later writing.

Developing a sense of audience

Because drama is often performed for others it is very powerful for seeing how our intended meanings are understood and interpreted. In many lessons, this may involve groups sharing their work with the rest of the class. Sometimes we may develop work in drama that we want to share in performance with the whole school or with parents and the community. When we do so, we need to think hard about what we want to say and how we want to say it. While the audience for our written work may be at some remove, audiences for this kind of performance are in the room with us and their response and feedback can be much more immediate. This can be particularly highlighted when children write play or film scripts. If children are asked to write scripts that others perform, they can be very surprised and intrigued by how their writing is developed and interpreted.

All of these elements and qualities of drama and role play combine to make a powerful contribution to the development of young writers, to the stock of stories they have experienced and have to tell, and to their use of spoken language which is the absolute foundation on which the written word is built. The examples that follow show how these elements might combine to offer rich experiences for children, some of which have writing built into the whole process, others which give children exciting and memorable imagined experiences which inform their subsequent writing.

Example 1: The florist

The children in this nursery have collaborated with the adults who work with them to set their role-play area up as a florist's shop. The opportunities for putting writing in context are immediate and plentiful: posters for the window; labels for the flowers; tickets with prices; advertisements; opening times; and order forms. Some of these are handwritten and combined with drawing, others are made using ICT. Quickly the

49

florist's shop is rich in both spoken and written language as customers come in, place their orders, talk to the shop assistants about the flowers they want, tell them about why they are buying flowers and for whom, and seek advice about what might be most suitable. Based on their observations, the adults make skilful interventions to sustain and extend the play: they know when to intervene and, just as importantly, when to leave well alone.

One of the adults then notices some differences in the engagement of different children. Most take part willingly and purposefully, but a minority seem to need something more to sustain and extend their interest. She goes into the shop, goes straight to the counter, and tells the shopkeeper that she has come about the job as the van driver. The child who is the shopkeeper quickly spots the possibility in this play, even though she wasn't aware that she had a vacancy. The selection procedure is brief to say the least. 'Can you drive a van?' she asks. 'Oh yes,' comes the reply. 'OK then, you need to take these flowers to 28 Winston Gardens.' Keeping in her role, and playing it with complete integrity, the adult asks for directions. When she is told, she expresses concern that she will forget and asks for the directions to be written down. Without hesitation the shopkeeper takes a pad and pencil and makes the necessary marks for the driver to know her way. The driver takes the piece of paper, reads the directions and nods that she understands but still asks if someone could come with her as this is her first trip. Another shop assistant goes with her and the story of the delivery driver begins. Soon everyone wants a go – directions are given out and taken to the van, orders brought back because they went to the wrong address, and phone calls are made to check details. Other children record directions onto a digital voice recorder which in turn becomes the satellite navigation system for the van. Once the van is part of the story of the flower shop, the indoor role-play area connects with outdoor play. One bouquet has to be taken to Scotland – a journey which takes only a minute or two in the imagined world of the story. And the florist's shop is as active and full of purposeful talk and writing as any real shop. In the midst of all the busy activity another adult rings up to place her order. She starts to tell the assistant what she wants when she is interrupted. 'Just a minute,' says the assistant, 'I need to write that down.' Though this shop assistant is not yet four, she already understands something of the power and importance of the written word. Most importantly of all, she is learning about this in a real, human context which she understands very well and in which she can act with expert confidence. It never occurs to her that she doesn't know what or how to write.

More than anything, the example of the florist's shop illustrates how writing can be an integral and natural part of children's play. Just as it often is in the adult world, writing is a necessary element of everyday work and young children accept it as naturally as they do any other element of the role they are playing. From this very early age, they can experience writing that is both purposeful and powerful.

Example 2: Jack and the Beanstalk

This is a very popular and well-known story in plenty of early years settings. It is often connected with work on living and growth with children growing their own beanstalks and making careful observations as they do so. But the story also delights children because of its playfulness with scale; like Jack in the story, they too are small people in a big world and they enjoy the exaggeration of that experience which is at the heart of the tale. Told well, the story is also delightfully dangerous.

The work in this Reception class begins with the teacher telling the first part of the story. As she does so, she asks children to come to the front and take on the characters' roles. She keeps the focus of the story on what Jack's mum sees and knows – she tells how Jack disappeared up the beanstalk and came back with some money, how he told her where he'd got the money and how she had made Jack promise not to go up the beanstalk again. Then she tells how Jack got up very early the next morning, well before his mother was awake, and climbed the beanstalk again. But, she adds, some of the other children who live in the same village as Jack were also up early – and they saw where he went.

Next, the teacher asks her class about the children who are Jack's friends – what do they do and where do they meet? They tell her that there is a playground in the village where they all go. The teacher asks the class to show her what the children do, and they mime playing games – she gives them very clear signals for playing and for 'freezing' the action. When the action is 'frozen' she talks about what she can see and the sorts of games the children play together.

Then the teacher takes a role in the story herself. She tells the class that she is going to be Jack's mum and that she will wear a shawl to show everyone that that is who she is. She sets the children playing, then puts on the shawl and asks the children if she can have a quick word. They come across to her, sit down, and she asks them if they have seen her Jack at all. The children eagerly tell her that he has gone up the beanstalk again. Jack's mum will not believe this, telling the children that Jack had promised not go again, but they eventually persuade her that it is true. Still in role as Jack's mum, the teacher tells the children that she is very worried about Jack but she does not think she would be able to climb the beanstalk to go and get him back – would they mind going for her? The children agree readily.

At this stage the teacher goes back into the role of narrator. As she tells the story the children mime with her. She tells of how they climb the beanstalk, how they reach the top and see a great castle in the distance, how they walk to the castle and summon up the courage to knock on the huge door. Briefly, she takes on a second role as the giant's wife. The children tell her they have come to get their friend back. She agrees to let them in but warns them about her husband: 'If you hear someone calling Fee Fi Fo Fum,' she tells them, 'You must hide as quickly as you can.' The teacher then takes a moment to practise 'hiding'. She tells the children that, rather than run and hide when they hear Fee Fi Fo Fum, they should make a 'hiding shape' in the space where they are working. Some curl up very small, others make themselves very thin, others make shapes to suggest they are peering over or under something. She encourages them to make a different shape each time they hide. Then she narrates again, telling how the children explore the castle, and the children act out the story with her. Every now and again she tells how the children could hear Fee Fi Fo Fum and they all 'hide'. Then she tells how, after they have hidden and come out again for the third time, the children find Jack. Quickly, she takes the role of Jack and asks what the children are doing there. When they tell Jack, he says that he is not coming down yet because he has found out that the giant stole most of what he has from Jack's father – will the children help him take it back? There is some considerable discussion, but the children eventually decide that it would be right to help Jack. Again, the teacher narrates how they take things from the giant, including his singing harp, how the harp calls to him and how he chases after the children. In this version, however, the children slam the door behind them as they leave and manage to turn the giant key, so locking in the giant. They climb down the beanstalk to safety and tell Jack's mum all about what happened. The teacher then leaves the story until tomorrow.

When the children arrive in school the next morning, the teacher has made a huge letter on a big sheet of flooring paper. It reads:

> Please let me out. I promise not to steal any more if you do.
> From the Giant

The teacher and the children talk together about how they should reply to the giant's letter. So begins a playful exchange which the teacher manages very skilfully, responding to the children's letters by preparing a new letter from the giant each morning. He complains that he is finding it difficult to read their letters because, to him, their writing is very small. The teacher tells the children that she has found what must be a giant's pencil at the foot of the beanstalk. She has made the 'pencil' from a broom handle with a large felt-tip pen fixed to the end and the children delight in experimenting with forming huge letters on big sheets of paper: for some of them, this is an important new opportunity to 'feel' how letters are formed on a bigger scale than usual.

They set their imaginative play area up as the giant's kitchen, experimenting with playful ways of making giant cups, bowls, knives and forks. Their play extends outside as they use huge bits of drain-pipe to make furniture for the giant. And all the time they are doing this, they use rich language as they work together and tell each other about the stories they are making.

The children in this class were led into this story by their teacher's careful blending of oral storytelling and drama. This allowed the children physically to experience the story as well as just hear it. The playful interaction of writing between the children and the giant had the same excited anticipation that accompanies the arrival of a real letter or email from friends and family. And the integration of their role and outdoor play extended the opportunities for talking and writing even further.

Example 3: The Elves and the Shoemaker

The teacher of this Year 2 class also begins the work with some storytelling. We have included his version in Appendix 2 because it has a number of variations on the Brothers Grimm original which become important as the drama develops with the children. This version makes specific reference to the shoemaker's failing eyesight as the root cause of his poverty. It also gives a rather different account of how he discovers the elves at work.

The teacher tells the story to the point where the shoemaker discovers the elves in his workshop. He finishes with a typical storyteller's question: And do you know what he saw? By this time the children are bursting to tell him what they know. They talk briefly about the jobs that the elves need to do and collect a list of verbs which include cutting, stitching, sewing, gluing, hammering and polishing. They also talk about scale – the elves are very small and the shoes they have to make are much bigger than their own. The children play with miming the big movements that the elves will have to do to make such big shoes.

This teacher uses a 'story stick'. It is just an old walking stick, but he and his class like to use the idea that the stick is full of stories – if you want to tell one, you need only hold on to the stick and the words will travel up your arm and out of your mouth. He also uses the stick to manage the drama by telling the children that when he taps the stick on the floor three times they are going be the elves at work in the shoemaker's workshop. If he holds the stick in the air and calls 'story stick!' they must stop in the middle of what they are doing. In this way he creates instant 'pictures' of the elves at work. He walks through the pictures, commenting on what he sees and talking to the elves about their work. He also takes pictures with a digital camera for the children to use in their subsequent writing. Next, he introduces a rhyme that the elves use to keep them working together. It goes:

Tap – tap, tap – tap, making shoes
Tap tap tap, no time to lose!

Then he turns the freeze/move structure into a game. It is important to the elves that they are not discovered, so they only work when the shoemaker is asleep. The teacher tells them that he is going to be the shoemaker and that when he is 'asleep' on the floor they can work, but if he wakes up they must stop immediately.

It is built into his version of the story that each night the elves must make more and more pairs of shoes, and that each night the shoemaker and his wife enjoy bigger and better suppers. So it is perfectly logical that one night when the shoemaker cannot sleep because he has eaten too much, the elves don't hear him get up and come to the workshop, because they have too much work to do. The teacher is about to take the role of the shoemaker and enact his discovery of the elves at work, but before he does so, he carefully negotiates with the children that the elves will not realise that the shoemaker is there until it is too late for them to run and hide – he is going to ask them to stop working and come and talk to him.

They enact their planned story together and the shoemaker calls the elves to come and talk. In these moments of live engagement between the shoemaker and the elves, the teacher uses his role to explore the story in much greater depth than he could ever achieve by sitting the children on the carpet and interrogating them. He plays his role with complete integrity and the children respond by talking to him just as if he is an old shoemaker and they are elves who have come to help him. This allows him to ask questions which they answer *in the first person*. Who are they? Why have they come to help him? How did they know about him? And unlike the 'guess what's in my head' quality which is characteristic of so much teacher questioning, the children happily accept that the shoemaker does not know and that they need to explain.

Then he asks a question which has stories pouring from the children – Have you ever helped anyone else? They respond eagerly with stories about the time they helped the baker, the tailor, even the policeman. The teacher uses his role to question and probe them about what they did and what happened – the teaching assistant is listening carefully to every word and capturing all that she can about the stories the children are making. Back in the classroom, they will begin work on a class anthology of *The Elves and the . . .* stories.

The shoemaker also asks the elves where they go when they are not out helping someone. Quite spontaneously, they tell all about their underground home. He asks if he would be able to visit, and one elf explains how she will work some magic so that he is small enough to go with them. Working entirely from their spontaneous imagination, the children show the shoemaker around: where they eat, where they sleep, where they meet together to talk and plan their next mission.

They turn their imaginative play area into the elves' meeting place. They hang tree roots from the ceiling, make toadstools to sit on, nutshells to drink from, but also include computers with which they can receive email messages and look around the world to see who needs help.

One morning the teacher leaves a letter for the elves to discover. It reads:

Grimm Farm
Mud Lane
Gloomshire
Email: meeny@cagetherabbits.com

Dear elves
Yesterday I met a shoemaker and he told me all about the help you gave him when he was so very poor. After I heard his story, it made me wonder whether you would mind coming over to help me in the same way.
   I own a great big farm where I keep lots of rabbits in cages. The trouble is, the rabbits keep getting out and running away. I've tried tying them up and making the cages as strong as possible, but they still keep getting away. Can you help me make some better cages so that they can't escape?
Yours truly,
Farmer Meeny

As the elves, the children start to talk about what they should do and whether Farmer Meeny deserves their help. They draft replies to his letter. Some of them reply by email, others improvise and record a phone call.

Then the teacher narrates: 'Then came something that had never happened to the elves before – someone came to see them in person.' He has a rabbit puppet and explains to the children that the rabbit is so afraid that she will only nod or shake her head in response to questions. The children have to work hard to frame closed questions in such a way as to get as much information as they can: Are you from Grimm Farm? Is Farmer Meeny mean to you? Do you need our help? Using the information they get from the rabbit, the elves begin to plan how they will rescue the rabbits and set them free. The teacher listens carefully and notes down their ideas. Ready for their next lesson, he prepares the story of the rescue using the ideas they have given. Using the story stick he tells the story of the rabbits' rescue. At one point he tells how the elves see the keys to the cages under the chair in which Farmer Meeny is asleep. He then builds a version of the game *Keeper of the Keys* into the story whereby different elves try to creep in and take the keys from under the sleeping farmer's chair. After each attempt, the children are encouraged to describe the way in which the elf and the farmer moved: the teaching assistant notes all their ideas down on large sheets of paper so that they can use them in their later writing. Like most stories for this age group, theirs has a happy ending in which Farmer Meeny is outwitted by the guile and stealth of the elves and the rabbits are set free.

Once the teacher has told the traditional story up the point where the shoemaker discovers the elves at work, the direction of the narrative is determined by the children's decisions and actions. They live the story together, and the living of that imagined experience is what inspires and supports so much writing: stories of how the elves help others; responses to requests for help; the story of rescuing the rabbits. It is a very rich and varied unit of work which fills children with ideas for stories and gives them plenty to write about.

Example 4: Queen Boudicca and the Iceni Uprising

This Year 4 class are looking at this story as part of their work in history. The teacher begins the drama by dividing the class into groups and giving each an extract which tells part of the story of the Iceni Uprising:

1. The Roman Conquest of Britain began in AD43. At this time, Britain was divided into tribes, one of which was the Iceni of East Anglia.
2. The Iceni were a client kingdom, one of the tribes the Romans allowed to keep their lands and govern themselves. But after the death of Boudicca's husband, King Prasutagus, in AD60, the Iceni came under full Roman rule.
3. Prasutagus left a will in which he promised half the Iceni kingdom to the Romans, and half to his widow, Boudicca. But the Romans ignored the will and seized the throne. They sacked Thetford, the Iceni capital, and publicly whipped Queen Boudicca and her two young daughters.
4. Determined to get revenge for her family, her tribe, and all Britons under Roman rule, Boudicca led a revolt.
5. The rebel army marched on Camulodunum, the Roman capital. They were joined by another tribe, so Boudicca's army now had around 100,000 men, women and children.
6. The rebels stormed Colchester, burning, looting and sacking the city.
7. Boudicca's army then marched south to Londinium. There were no Roman soldiers in the city because they were needed elsewhere in Britain. The city was burned to the ground and everyone in it was slaughtered.
8. After sacking London, the army headed north, looking for the Roman legions.

To begin with, the teacher asks the children to prepare a still image (or tableau) to represent their part of the story. When the class see these images in turn, they already begin to speculate about the story that lies behind, even though no group knows the whole of it. They use large sheets of paper to record words and phrases from these first impressions.

Then the teacher asks them to add words and movement so that they begin with one still, move and speak briefly, then finish with another still. She gives them the constraint that no group can use more than ten words in total – these may be spoken by one character, or perhaps by the whole group together. It is the kind of constraint which encourages creativity, and the children cleverly subvert it by, for example, repeating the same word several times and only counting it as one of their words. The resulting combination of still and moving images makes a very concentrated and very beautiful representation of the story – the teacher insisting that they move from one group's work to another's without any extraneous talk or movement. It takes two or three goes to get it right, but the outcome is well worth it. The children now have a rich understanding of the story which they got by engaging with it physically. They have also collected words and phrases which they will use in their subsequent writing.

Their teacher has found them some translated extracts from Tacitus which describe the sacking of Colchester. She reads these aloud to the children and asks them to notice and write down phrases that they think are particularly powerful. Then she asks each group to devise three tableaux based on what they have heard. Moving between the groups as they work, she encourages variation and precision in the images. Then she asks the children to devise movements from the first image to the second, the second to the third, and the third back to the first. When the movements are well practised, she asks the children to add words and phrases to them based on what they noticed from the Tacitus readings. Tableaux, movement and words then combine to make a powerful representation of the sacking which the children find exciting and challenging to create – it is also very hard work to perform. As soon as they have been through their stills, movements and words a dozen or so times without interruption, she gives them large sheets of paper and encourages them to write as much as they can about what they saw, did and felt. Some groups immediately begin to form their responses into poetry; others will take key words and phrases back to the classroom for further crafting.

The teacher then wants the children to write in the first person giving an account of how they felt on the eve of the battle between Boudicca's army and the Romans. She divides the class in two, one half to represent the Romans, the other the Britons. Then they take time to plan and perform soundscapes for each other. These are a combination of the thoughts that might be going through a soldier's head and the sounds and cries of the anticipated battle. To begin with, the children tend to make a cacophony which deafens from beginning to end, but the teacher encourages them to use more variation and subtlety, recognising that silence can be at least as terrifying as loud noise. The resulting soundscapes are very powerful and lead straight into the children finding a quiet space where they can sit and write their own diary entry from the eve of battle.

Of course these children know nothing of the real terror of battle – we would not want them to. But the drama they undertook actively supported the process of imagining and writing how it might have been. They were deliberately enabled to bring all their senses to that process of imagining – no one said that they did not know what to write.

Example 5: Living in the Wild Wood

This Year 6 class have been reading *The Wind in the Willows*. They have enjoyed it, but have become particularly interested in the characters who live in the Wild Wood. They begin by talking about the ways in which they are described in Kenneth Graeme's original text. They list the words and phrases he uses, then make a second list of words which the Wild Wooders might use to describe themselves: cunning, crafty, watchful, loyal, fun-loving. These words are used to develop tableaux that subsequently move and speak phrases that begin with 'A Wild Wooder should be . . .'. Their work is very playful and an image emerges of a group that look after each other and are very streetwise – they coin the term 'woodwise'. The class then stand in a circle and use rhythmic clapping and stamping as each of their images is brought in turn to the centre of the circle. The clapping and stamping stops while the words and movements are performed, and then starts again to accompany the last group out of the circle and the next one in. Already, this is beginning to feel like a Wild Wood ritual where the animals come together to celebrate who they are and what they do.

Rituals often include food, and the class begin to talk about the sorts of food that the Wild Wooders might enjoy. They collect menus from local pubs and restaurants and from the internet and begin to explore the ways in which food is described. They particularly enjoy collecting verbs like drizzled, glazed and sautéed, and noticing dishes that are described as compote or frappé. Each group devises its own way of describing what they will bring to the ritual – they also rehearse a way of miming its presentation with the words 'We bring . . .'. So, for example, one group says, 'We bring pan-roasted mice, glazed with elderflower syrup and served with crushed hazel nuts'. The circle is re-formed and the bringing of food is now added to the ritual, with the Wild Wooders enthusiastically applauding each dish as it is put before them.

The teacher borrows from Jan Needle's book *Wild Wood* the idea that the animals are also great brewers. She has a stone jar in which, she tells the class, is kept the first of this year's brew. The jar is brought to the circle and left in the middle for a few moments. The teacher narrates that it is a tradition of the Wild Wood that at this point any member of the community may come in and pick up the jar – if they do so, they must be heard without interruption. She adds that this is an important custom, but that nobody has actually picked the jar up for as long as anyone can remember.

The class put their ritual together, combining their 'A Wild Wooder should be . . .' images with their ritual clapping and stamping and the mimed presentation of their food. The stone jar is taken to the middle, then the teacher narrates that this year someone does come and pick it up. She walks to the middle, picks up the jar and starts talking to the other Wild Wooders. She apologises to them for keeping them from their food, but explains that they must talk urgently about the behaviour of Mr Toad. She tells how his latest obsession with cars is endangering some of the young animals who like to play at the edges of the wood – one of her own children was almost killed by his car the other day. A heated discussion ensues about what should be done.

Over the next two to three weeks, the class engages in an extended writing project in which they tell the story from the perspective of the Wild Wooders – how they hear about Toad's arrest and how they plan the capture of Toad Hall. As they do so, the teacher combines elements of drama, detailed research from the original text, and carefully structured teaching to explore and achieve particular effects. Working over this extended period, and having their imagination supported by well-planned drama, makes it possible for these children to produce writing at length in which they take genuine pride.

The five examples we have set out here use a range of drama strategies appropriate to different age groups. What they have in common is that children are very active in the making of their stories, they are supported by making them collectively, and the teachers make the links with writing explicit. Of course it takes a certain level of skill and confidence to work in this way, but there are plenty of books and courses to help you develop this. What we find with so many of the teachers with whom we work is that once they develop the confidence to try combining drama and writing in these ways, neither they nor the children they teach want to stop.

5 | Using sounds and images

As we explored in Chapter 3, good writing by good authors can provide a powerful stimulus and excellent models for children's writing. Many effective writing lessons rely primarily on a chosen text as their stimulus.

Yet we have all met children who find it hard to believe in their ability as a writer because they think that to be able to do their own writing, they have to be good at reading the writing of others. If a child is a reluctant reader, it seems to follow that they must be a reluctant writer. But this does not have to be the case. We have found that you can challenge a breadth of ability if you are brave and creative enough to experiment with images, sound and movement. There can be real value in initiating a writing activity other than by using text as a stimulus; indeed, the new Literacy Framework emphasises the need to engage all the senses, immersing children in a more holistic writing experience. Interestingly, the children who often find this most challenging are the more able, as children who often struggle suddenly feel more liberated and discover an articulate voice they never realised they had. So why should this be?

Music and art can give us the power to think, feel and question. Their language is universal, yet we respond to it as individuals. These creative forms evoke reactions which are often quite passionate; reactions that encourage us to ask questions, find reasons, make decisions, and speak.

Using sounds

In our babbling as babies we make our first exploration of human sounds. During this first stage of development, you can hear children discovering the incredible range of sound and textures that their voices can create. Poets never stop. They are acutely aware of the effect that sound can have on the way a phrase is illustrated in our minds. There is an obvious link between music and the spoken word – rhythm, pattern, intonation, pitch, moments of silence. But written words can also hum with musicality, enriching the reading experience either silently or aloud. Developing an awareness of the melody in language can be rewarding and productive, and it demands that we play with words. Encouraging children to investigate the fascinating relationship between sound and language can lead them to a deeper understanding of its effects and enliven their writing. When evocative sounds are combined with carefully chosen images, children can respond with imagination, confidence and enthusiasm.

Tuning in to sounds

Many teachers will recognise that one of the biggest barriers to developing confidence in children as writers is their fear of spelling. They can be terrified of writing a word incorrectly, not least because most forms of writing that are put in front of them are immaculate. The pages of their reading book are examples of intimidating perfection: perfectly formed letters hang in perfect rows, though there are not even any lines to hang them on. There are no crossings out or blotches. To expect to write creatively with such crispness and precision is something that not even the greatest professional writers can achieve. Children need to be able to share more examples of the starting point for real writers – their sketchy drafts, their scrawled ideas captured on the backs of envelopes. But this also means that at the very earliest stage of writing we want children to become confident scribblers, doodlers and mark makers. We need to provide opportunities for them to make marks in a variety of ways and these marks should not be exposed to the correction pen. They should be means of expression that enable children to record what they see and hear in their heads.

Music is an excellent stimulus for expressive mark making. Once the children have become musical doodlers, they can lose their fear of making mistakes and become more attuned to the rhythm and pattern of words.

The following simple activities will help to raise children's awareness of sounds that are all around them. As soon as they begin to pick out and appreciate sounds, they will be collecting language that can be used effectively in their writing. Towards the end of this chapter, we give suggestions for ways to enrich writing by combining the imagery of sounds and pictures.

Example 1: Making sound symbols

The following activity releases children of all the anxiety that surrounds capturing an idea on paper. To begin with the children will learn to read and interpret musical symbols, not words. Then they will be drawing out their own musical language, which will be in the form of big, exciting symbols. Eventually, this is linked with written words and, as a result, the children are armed with a rich vocabulary for further writing activities.

Resources

- Flip chart paper and pens (for teacher).
- A space big enough for children to sit down in a circle.
- A3 paper (two pages per child) and chunky pens.
- Musical instruments – one per child.

Step one

Before you ask children to interpret sound symbols, they need to have an understanding of the dynamics of sound; pitch, volume and texture. This can be developed through a simple introductory activity.

Press your hands together (in a praying shape) and hold them central to your body at waist height. Explain to the children that this is the signal to stop. When you open up your hands this is the signal to make any sound they want to with their voices. Make sure you make a sound too, as the children will be unsure to begin with. It need only be a simple hum. Don't be afraid of unusual responses, and don't worry that they won't all be on the same note. They will produce a wonderful, haunting sound.

Now explain that as your hands move further away the sound gets louder, as they move closer to the starting and finishing (praying) position, the sound becomes quieter.

Allow your hands to move higher and lower. Explain that this changes pitch; how high or low their voices go.

Slowly draw shapes with your finger (as you would when the children are learning letters). Allow the children to follow and interpret what sound this might make as they follow with their fingers. A wavy shape will create undulating pitch. Stabbing the air with your finger will be a staccato note; short, sharp and detached, a surprise note (like an exclamation mark). How high or low the note is will depend on where you point.

Start to think about the emphasis that you use on the shapes you are making with your hands.

Now that children are starting to visualise sound, they are ready to interpret sound symbols.

Step two

The previous activity and the next allow children to explore the shape of sounds, which will stand them in good stead when learning about the shape of language.

This time, instead of making shapes with your hands, you are going to have some ready prepared 'sound shapes' (see Figure 5.1). These are straightforward symbols that do the same job that your hands did in the last exercise.

Point to the start of the symbol and ask the children to follow the image, making the sound of the image with their voices. They can interpret it any way they want to. Don't be afraid of the diverse responses you will hear. The children will see the symbols differently; there is no wrong and no right. There is only a beginning and an end and you must make it clear that at the end of the symbol the children should stop the sound. Figure 5.1 shows some examples of symbols and possible interpretations.

You can use a mixture of symbols, some that can explore pitch (how high or low their voices will be), some that will explore texture.

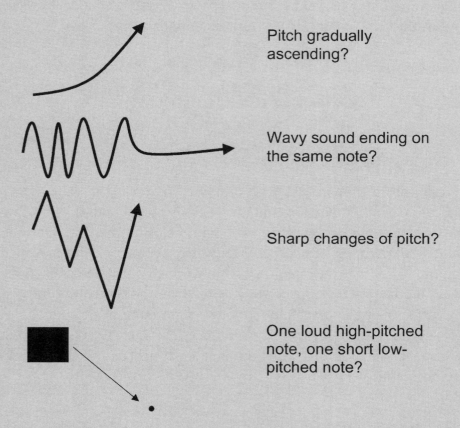

Pitch gradually ascending?

Wavy sound ending on the same note?

Sharp changes of pitch?

One loud high-pitched note, one short low-pitched note?

Figure 5.1 Examples of sound symbols

Step three

You will now want the children to start creating their own 'musical language' by drawing symbols, which will be created from the sounds of musical instruments. But before you do, you will need to establish a sense of respect for instruments in your classroom. Simply ask the children to sit in a circle, then, choosing a particularly noisy instrument like a tambourine or a shaker, ask the children to pass the instrument around the circle without making a sound. After a minute or so, you can send another instrument around in the opposite direction, so someone has to cross over in the middle. The children will be sitting very still and listening intently. They will probably be holding their breath! You are emphasising that silence is as important as sound in music making, just as rhythm and pause are effective in writing.

Tell the children that they are to have one instrument each, and on this instrument they must make three different gentle sounds. The challenge is to make soft sounds that are not the same. If you are working on a particular theme you could relate the sounds to this – for example, the children might make three soft sea sounds.

Ask the children to draw symbols for the sounds they have made. Let them have large sheets of paper and big pens, so their arms can make wide, confident sweeps across the page. All of this is helping them to lose inhibitions with writing.

Ask them to leave their music (for that is what it is) next to their instruments and move to someone else's. They must read another person's music and play it on the new instrument.

How this process builds confidence in writing

What is powerful about this process is that their mark making is being read without question and turned into interesting sounds. How many children do we know that cannot bear to share their written work with the next child because when they read it out it sounds awkward and wrong? Or even worse, the other child may claim (probably quite loudly) that they can't read the writing or that the spelling is all wrong? One of the hardest jobs for a writer is to share their work with other people. This activity turns writing into something quite empowering. It celebrates diverse written responses. There is no wrong and no right. The work is not marked, but all work has a response, and all responses are unique. It echoes the relationship between real writers and real readers.

How this process leads to writing

Eventually, the children should return to their own symbols and instruments. They should now pick their favourite, draw it out again – even bigger – and this time write words around it that describe the sound that it makes. Sometimes this description might just be a letter sound like 'sh'; this should be encouraged as children are linking sounds to graphemes. Quantity is important here and children should be writing down as many ideas as they can, talking to others, finding out how people who played their symbols interpreted the sounds, listing as many words as they can. The pictorial form will also challenge and inspire them – it may not otherwise occur to them that sounds can be wavy or scratchy, and encouraging this sort of interpretation can, in turn, encourage originality in young writers.

Example 2: Sound story

If we want children to recognise that they have the ability to tell stories, we need to teach them to notice the fragments of stories that are happening all around them. Sound is an important element in descriptive writing. It is a wonderful way of building suspense and affecting the emotions of the reader.

In this activity, the children will learn to recognise the 'sound story' of a setting, by becoming more aware of sounds in their own location. They will think about where these sounds are positioned in the room. Finally, they will use their imagination to create sounds for a setting from a book, map it out and then use this stimulus for inspiration in writing.

Resources

- A selection of everyday objects.
- A selection of instruments.

Step one

In this first stage, children will be at their desks, with paper on which they can jot and scribble ideas.

Explain that the sounds you hear around a space tell you a story about where you are. For example, the whirr of the photocopier tells us that we are near to the office, the creak of the poplar trees tells us that we are in the mobile classroom, and so on.

Ask the children to close their eyes. They must listen to what they hear around them. If this was a recording and you were somewhere else, could you use the recording to identify where the sounds took place?

While the children have their eyes closed, the teacher makes three different sounds from items in the room. It could be the sound of water pouring out of the tap, a desk lid opening, a board rubber erasing words. Children open their eyes and quickly write down what might have made the sounds.

Step two

Now the children can get up and move around. This is important – too much sitting down can hinder the writing process.

Having moved into pairs, the children identify something in the room whose sound contributes to the story of the space. For example, a door handle, a child's work tray, a whiteboard pen being opened. They are allowed to gently move their chosen object to create a sound.

After the children have had time to move their object and experiment with its sound, stop them, so you have silence. Explain that creating silence at the beginning is imperative to any good performance. Talk to the children about their sound. Explain to them that they will have a chance to play it within the class group as part of a performance. They need to think about whether it should play all the way through because it is rhythmic, whether is should be played intermittently because it is atmospheric, or whether they should choose a couple of key moments because it is surprising. Remind them that they do not have to start when signalled, they can choose to wait, but they must have finished by the final signal. Indicate that the music will probably last no longer than one minute, so the children have some idea of when the time will run out.

Signal the children to start. There should be no talking (unless children have chosen this as a sound). Children then perform the story of the room through sound.

Teachers we have worked with are often surprised by the power of this exercise. Children are incredibly careful and controlled about the way they play and when the activity is followed with discussion, pupils use vivid language to describe the sounds they have made. One Year 5 child described a 'wincing door handle'. Indeed, the handle was squeaking so sharply that the boy felt it winced every time it was levered. It gave the handle a character, it started to have its own story. Without doing this exercise and listening so attentively, it is unlikely that he would have thought of this. The next step is to apply this exercise to a text you are using.

Step three

Now that the children are aware of what sounds tell us about a setting, they will be ready to create a soundscape from a real or fictional setting.

Use a picture or a written description of a setting as a stimulus. Ask children to observe it closely and think about what would be needed to tell a sound story about this place.

Organise the children into groups and assign a different area of the setting for them to re-create, or give them different settings from the same story. For example, if you were reading *The Lady of Shallot* one group might make sounds for the river, another the road winding down to Camelot, another the 'fields of barley and of rye'.

Tell the children that you are going to give them some instruments that should tell the sound story of the setting they are exploring. Explain that they will be given time to experiment with the resources they are given. Teachers can be really creative here. You don't necessarily have to give them musical instruments. For example, different qualities of paper can create incredible sounds either through rubbing, crunching, ripping, waving or even sliding along the floor. We recently did this with a group of Year 3 children who were studying 'The Iron Man': as he is such a mechanical, industrial character, they were given lots of kitchen utensils which made metallic sounds, such as whisks and spoons.

Step four

The next stage is to collect the sounds and turn them into words. The teacher will need to have a large board or piece of paper, where different areas of the setting are mapped. The features should be indicated by name rather than sound.

Children are given time to reflect and remember sounds they have made and heard from other groups where they were in the room. Give them two minutes to list as many sounds as they can remember. After this they can look again at their list. Allow them time to adapt their list if they wish, using a thesaurus to extend or improve on words they have used.

Children are given self-adhesive notes. Looking back at their improved list, they pick out their favourite words and phrases, trying to choose one from each sound area. Using one note for each idea, they should write down the word(s) and then stick the note where the sound should be on the map.

How this process builds confidence in writing

Having to explore ways of making the sounds in the setting inspires children to think of more original ideas to describe things. For example, using a metallic instrument to simulate the sound of the sea over the pebbles and rocks might create a 'creaking' sound. Without actually making the sound first, reluctant writers might use a word like 'stormy'. Now that the class has a map of evocative sound words, there are a number of ways they can be used for writing.

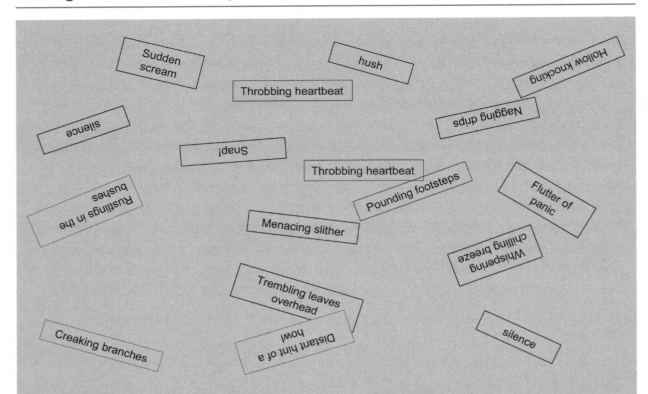

Figure 5.2 Example of a sound map from 'Red Riding Hood'

How this process leads to writing

Organise the children into groups. Then 'word pick': pick a selection of self-adhesive notes for each group, ensuring that there are notes from every section, and put them in a box. Each group empties out their box and looks carefully at the words. For example, a Year 5 group we worked with had 'whispering', 'creaking', 'scraping', 'crunching', 'swishing'. Give the children five minutes to choose nouns to go with the words. Our Year 5 children then had 'whispering sea', 'creaking rocks', 'scraping seagulls', 'seaweed swishing'. Then give them five minutes to add more character or feeling to the words. The Year 5 group then wrote 'friendless whispering sea', 'sinister creaking rocks', 'scavenging scraping seagulls', 'licking seaweed swishing'. The children will then want to take these lines and adapt them, swap word order so that it sounds better, omit words, improve them, add them. A further step is to define a main 'character' and link the other images to this character. Our Year 5 group finished with this:

> Can you hear
> The friendless sea?
> It whispers into emptiness,
> Cowering behind forgotten secrets of creaking rocks
> It opens up its hidden depths to scavenging gulls.
> Seaweed tongues lick at lost treasures.

Can you hear the sea?
The friendless sea?
It whispers into emptiness.
Yet the sea is full.

Poems are often written to be performed, so there are lots of opportunities for children to feel that their writing will be valued. It could be that the children recite their poems in an assembly or at a school poetry festival. They would want to consider how they might produce the best effect in performance – where will they want to stand? Would they like to stand around the outside of the audience? Would they like the audience to have their eyes closed? Would they be scattered among the audience? Could they enhance the words by using instrumental sounds?

Other ways that this process can lead to writing

Come together as a group. Explain that the children are going to be making a pilot radio recording for a possible radio station that might be available to their parents. They are to imagine they are producing a report of the setting they have been working on for radio. Speaking into a digital voice recorder, model for the children how the words they have used can be a stimulus for talk. You can make mistakes on purpose, so the children recognise the necessity for further note-taking to provide a structure for more organised talk. Model the note-taking.

It will help if you can map out the setting in a big open space like the hall, with all the words the children have gathered grouped appropriately. Organise the children into pairs or groups. Allow them to use their work in the hall to help them make decisions. Ask the children to make the recordings outdoors, so that authentic sounds can be heard.

Example 3: Change the sound

This process begins with a very quick and simple game, where children are encouraged to listen for sounds changing – a fundamental skill when learning to spell. As the activity progresses, there are opportunities to link the game to phonics and spelling and to produce imaginative sound effects that reflect a setting from a class text.

Resources

A space big enough to form a circle.

Step one

The whole class forms a circle. The teacher claps a slow, constant beat: clap clap, clap. All the children join in. When you are sure that the children are all in time, change the rhythm (e.g. clap-clap, clap. clap-clap, clap). Then again – stamp, clap-clap, stamp, stamp, etc. Now the children will be used to following, repeating and changing rhythms. Ask for a volunteer to be the leader. Give some of the pupils a chance to have a go at changing the rhythm for the class.

The teacher chooses a child (the 'guesser') to be sent out of the space. In a while, they will return to the circle, but for now, they should be out of sight and out of earshot. The teacher then chooses a child in the circle who will change the rhythm (the 'leader').

The teacher begins the rhythm with a slow, constant clap, which the children join in with. The guesser is invited to return and stand in the centre of the circle. They have to guess who is changing the rhythm.

The chosen child swaps the rhythm as the other children in the circle follow. But for those children following (and trying to fool the guesser) it is not just as simple as looking at the person changing the rhythm – this will give it away. If, for example, they are standing next to the leader, they will have to follow the person standing opposite them, or simply be more finely attuned to using their senses.

Step two – phonics

This game can be used effectively with younger children to practise phonetic sounds. There are several ways this can be done.

Instead of changing clapping rhythms, use phonemes. The teacher holds up sound cards. The child changing the rhythm decides when they will change to the new sound. For example, it could be the sound 'ch'. The children don't make the sound 'ch' until the chosen child begins to chant it. This tests the knowledge of an individual child (you would usually pick someone who is quite confident), while the rest of the group get the opportunity to practise and repeat.

Step three – spelling

For older children, this is a great alternative to a 'spelling bee'. More able spellers can be stretched, while those who need more practise benefit from the repetition and the slow buildup of letters.

Choose a word for the children to spell. The leader spells out the word gradually, by changing the letter. For example, they might spell out the word 'battle'. The leader starts by repeatedly calling out the letter 'b' while the rest of the group repeat. When he or she is sure that the guesser is not looking, he or she changes to 'a'. The object is to finish the word before the guesser finds the leader.

Step four

Choose a setting from a story or a poem you are reading. For example, it could be 'the purple moor' in 'The Highwayman'. You might even choose a still from a film, such as *Kirikou and the Sorceress*.

Instead of changing rhythm, children change sound – so they are creating a soundscape related to the setting, such as trees whistling, snakes slithering, etc. For example, a Year 2 'leader' started off with a 'ssss' noise, then changed to a blowing noise. The game becomes more difficult and enjoyable when actions are added to the sounds. So our Year 2 girl made wavy shapes with her hands as she made the 'ssss' sound, then shivery shapes with her shoulders for the blowing noise. Movement raises the energy levels and makes it more fun, and the followers have to be even more attentive, while it becomes more difficult for the guesser to pick out exactly where the change is happening.

How can this process develop confidence in writing?

We worked with a group of Year 1 children who did this. They were doing 'Under the Sea' as their theme. The leader started off with a 'shhh' sound. The other children followed. He then made a 'hhhh' sound and added actions with his shoulders. The other children followed.

When the game was finished, we recalled the sounds that had been used by the leader. The children did this individually as two scatter lists. They thought of words that described the sounds. For example, our Year 1 leader made the sound 'shhh'. The class decided that this was the sea shimmering. His next sound was 'hhhh'. The children said this was the sea breathing.

When we worked with the Year 1 children, we introduced a parachute at this point. We picked out all the sounds and words that the children used, and then used the parachute to simulate how the sea might appear for each one. The teaching assistant took photographs of each example.

These photographs were transferred to computers so that each child had access to them. The children worked with their computer partner, so they were able to discuss the work they produced and bounce ideas off each other. They then added words to go with the images: This is the morning sea breathing. . . . Sometimes the sea is angry. Here you can see it roaring.

Example 4: Word orchestra

Like the last process, this begins with a quick activity, which is easy to play, yet very adaptable. The children will each have their own instrument and will only play at the conductor's request. When the game is linked to a setting in a text, eventually sounds are swapped for poetic language and the resulting performance is a spontaneous, effective illustration of the power of words.

Resources

- Objects that make sounds, e.g. kitchen utensils, paper bags, children's voices.
- A 'soundscaping wand' (e.g. a beater).

Step one

Discuss a setting in a story, for example, the forest in *A Midsummer Night's Dream*. As a class, move into a circle, and reflect for a moment on what sounds might be present in the setting.

Give the children two minutes to explore how they could create this sound. As we mentioned earlier, paper or even paper bags make wonderful instruments in this type of exercise.

Step two

The teacher explains that they are the 'soundscaper', and when their 'wand' is pointed directly above their head, there is silence. They also explain that silence is as important as sound in creating tension and effect.

Using the 'wand', the teacher conducts sounds by pointing to children individually or picking out groups of sounds. It is best for the teacher to develop their own signs for conducting the children, but some starter suggestions are listed below.

> ABOVE HEAD: Silence/stop
> DIRECT POINT: Individual child plays using own expression
> LEFT TO RIGHT: Group of children
> UP AND DOWN: Children follow specific rhythm
> HANDS GRADUALLY WIDENING: Crescendo
> HANDS GRADUALLY CLOSING: Decrescendo

Step three

Children think about the sound they have made, then replace it with a descriptive word. A thesaurus could be used. The class can then be grouped like an orchestra – for alliterative sounds, rhythmic/polysyllabic words, soft sounds, plosives, and so on.

This is again conducted by a teacher or a pupil. The teacher can play around with poetic themes, such as repetition, alliteration and pace. It can be an exciting, spontaneous form of performance poetry, because there is a wonderful showering and layering of words.

How this process builds confidence in writing

In terms of performance, this game is instantly powerful because it sounds so amazing so quickly. But it isn't just about making a noise. Children will have heard language being layered all around them and will have picked up on the beauty of sound in the words. They will have absorbed a wealth of vocabulary, rhythmically balanced, which will enable them to write a poem, almost instantly, based on what they have heard. In a playful way, it highlights how writers choose language for dramatic impact and effect, based on sound.

Ways with images

We make choices about pictures we hang on the wall or the style of music we listen to based on personal taste. Even those of us who may never venture into an art gallery may be moved by a photograph in a newspaper, a picture in a magazine, or an image on the television. As we listen, sense or look, we create meanings and form opinions. The following suggestions show how we can use visual images creatively to get children looking, exploring, talking, thinking and writing.

Image activity 1: Catching a picture in your hand

Resources

- A corner of a room with lots of space that children can move in and out of (ideally in a hall).
- An overhead projector (if your school is in the process of throwing away your overhead projectors, save them as quickly as you can! Despite advances in whiteboard technology, OHPs can provide an approach to viewing images that is nothing short of magical).

The activity

Imagine that you are studying the evacuation of children from London in 1939 and you want to introduce the topic by provoking lots of discussion, and provide opportunities for exciting writing right at the start. Take an interesting black and white photograph, an image where there is a lot to see (such as refugees arriving at a train station). Make sure this is copied on to an acetate sheet of A4 size so it can be projected effectively.

Rather than projecting this image on to a whiteboard or flat surface, let the image spread into the corner of a room. Let it spill up on to the ceiling and catch on the walls and work surfaces. The children will not be able to see the image perfectly to begin with. In order to view it, they will need to take a blank piece of A3 paper, hold it up, step into the path of the projection and catch parts of the image on this paper. It is almost like exploring the picture with a large magnifying glass and because the detail is magnified, children will notice things that they would not have otherwise seen in a smaller picture. For example, you might see how the station master is wearing a big, cheery smile, but if you examine his eyes, they are far from smiling. You can see the tiny girl at the back with her sad, lost expression. You can see the brother and sister striding purposefully along the platform wearing fixed grins of excited anticipation, but you can also move your paper to study their small hands, gripped in painful togetherness. These hands tell a very different story from their sunny faces.

Observing a picture in this way highlights the paradoxes, the contradictions. It heightens the emotion and atmosphere in the picture. This, of course, instantly engages pupils in rich opportunities for challenge and discussion.

How this can lead to writing

No matter how large your projected image, the best way to get children to explore it is to divide the class into two halves. Each child needs a partner, so that when they go to view the picture, catching it on the paper, their partner sits on the outside, noting what they have found. As the children explore the projection, the image shows on both sides of their paper, and the people who are sitting out of the picture, a little further away, perceive different qualities from those who are close up. When it is time for the first partner to step out of the picture, you need to provide two minutes (limit the time so the children are keen to write) to allow the children to write down the images that they have noticed. Before you start, ask the children to call out some examples, and model the jotting process:

> jolly smiles
> eyes filled with emptiness
> two hands, tightly gripped

The children will then know that they don't have to write in long sentences, but the few words they use can be effective and powerful.

Further developments

There are many ways that you can adapt this idea. For example, when showing the evacuee picture, we have played different recordings in the background. The first is a typically jolly example of 1930s band music, of the sort that might accompany newsreels in the cinema. On the surface, this makes the people in the picture look brave and resilient, proud to be serving their country's cause. Then we have played a recording of the Queen as a young girl, speaking directly to her contemporaries who have left their mothers and fathers for the first time. Suddenly the picture becomes altogether more fragile. This exercise emphasises the importance of searching beneath the surface to find further truths – qualities we expect in good analytic readers, but also a necessity for writers who are keen observers of the subtleties of human behaviour.

Image activity 2: Stepping into an image

Overhead projection can be used quite imaginatively if the image is made really big and cast on to a wall or even a floor. Children can then step into the image, initially forming a tableau, then when prompted (and carefully controlled) can come to life and move inside it. For example, a group of Reception children we worked with 'stepped in' to a picture of Chinese New Year Celebrations. Children stepped in one by one or in pairs. Six children linked together in the middle to form the dragon. The others were a mixture of observers, little dogs, and one child even chose to be a kimono. The prompt for them to move within the picture was some Chinese music. This was enough for them to think about just how they should move within the space. It worked particularly well because the children had a good understanding and background knowledge of what was in the scene.

For older children, this activity provides opportunities for them to jot down responses about their physical and emotional reactions to character and place. A Year 4 class used it to help them think about the streets of Pompeii. They stepped into a projected photograph of how the streets look today. The large projection made the width of the streets almost as wide as their actual size. Children were able to use their knowledge of Ancient Rome to superimpose a tableau on to the modern picture, transforming the scene.

Image activity 3: Using one moving image

Resources

- Moving images of a simple setting saved on PowerPoint or similar (with sound). This could be an image of rain falling, an image of the sea, an image of a river. Many of these can be downloaded from the internet. You can also record them yourself on a digital camera.
- A data projector (preferably a portable one).
- A selection of objects to go with the scene.
- Self-adhesive notes.

Starting point – prepare the setting for the children

Let us say, for example, that you want the children to think about the rain. Get a video image of rain falling. If you have a portable data projector, let this image spill on to the floor. If not, project the image on to the whiteboard as usual, but make sure there is plenty of space in front of it so that the children can move around. Place objects in front of the image: umbrellas; Wellington boots; maybe even a picnic set; things that make children ask questions and think about consequences. Make sure the image has a good accompanying sound.

The children enter the space

When the children first come in, don't let them hear or see the image. Just let them look at the objects. Give them one minute to jot down ideas on scrap paper about anything it makes them think about. Some children may just list what they see, others may make connections, and others may ask questions.

Next, play the sound. Invite the children to move around the image, then give them another minute to jot down their feelings and reactions. Finally, play the image as well as the sound. Again, give the children one minute to record their reactions.

The reason that children should be allowed to jot down their reactions in between each stage is not only that they will want to express how they feel about the space, but also because their feelings will change with each introduction of object, sound and image.

How this process leads to writing

The last part is the element children usually enjoy most – the opportunity to ask anything they want about the scene. Use self-adhesive notes and allow the children to write one question per note. At their leisure they can go up and stick their notes to the appropriate part of the scene. This leads into opportunities for child-initiated learning tasks – as a class you can pursue certain questions that have been asked.

Image activity 4: Using an art gallery as a stimulus for writing

Inspiring children to write about a wonderful picture before they even get to the gallery can certainly get them almost as excited about visiting the art as visiting the shop!

Starting point – art word association

Organise the children into groups of three or four. Present one child with a postcard of a picture from the gallery you are going to visit. Tell them that they are not allowed to show anyone this picture.

Ask them to think of a word that says something about the picture they are looking at. For example, if the children were looking at the Mona Lisa, they might just say 'smile'. After they have said the first word, they will then become the scribe for their group. They are still not allowed to reveal the picture.

Each person then offers a word that is associated with the previous one. For example, in response to the word 'smile', another child might say 'warm', the next might say 'sun'.

Eventually there will be a list of interesting language, generated from one picture and one word. Ask the children to add other words to those they already have. Remind them that they can use nouns, adjectives, verbs and adverbs. For example, they might write:

> Sad smile
> Warm skin
> Angry sun

They are still not allowed to share the picture.

Finally give them a set time (about four minutes) to take their phrases and organise them in an order that they feel happy with. In a very short time, they will have produced a poetic form which is economic with language yet rich in meaning.

The next development is to share the picture with the whole group. When the children read their poem and look at the picture, they immediately analyse what they are looking at and hearing. How does it match? What does it mean? Which part of the picture does the poem lead us to and where does it take us? Does it take us beyond the picture?

We have used this approach with a group of children who were going to visit the British Folk Art Collection at Compton Verney Art Gallery in South Warwickshire. It would be hard to find a group of nine-year-olds anywhere who were more excited about going to view some paintings, because they wanted to find the paintings that they had written about. They wanted to know how the pictures were transformed when they were full-size and they could see the marks of the paintbrush. Would their poems become even more meaningful? As we stood in front of the original works with each group reading their own work, a hush filled the room. And as passers-by tuned into their readings, the children got the feeling that they were real writers, having something true and important to share with whoever would listen.

6 | Creating a range of texts

When we go to work in a school on *Click, Clack, Moo*, the story we explored in Chapter 3, we take a typewriter with us. It is a toy typewriter which was bought in the 1960s and has survived with its case and instruction leaflet intact. The instruction leaflet is strikingly different from anything one might expect to find with a new toy today. There are around 1200 words of description and instruction, a couple of diagrams and two black and white pictures. Instructions for one of the most popular construction toys in the world now have no words at all and rely entirely on a numbered sequence of brightly coloured photographs. There may be several reasons for this, not least that it allows the same leaflet to be included with the toy wherever in the world it might be sold. What is clear though, is that if we only teach children that instructions must include a written statement of the intended goal or outcome, a list of the materials needed, followed by the steps required to achieve it, we are simply misleading them. The types of text people create, their purposes, and the media used to create them are in a constant state of change.

For the teacher of writing in the primary school, these changes can present some profound challenges, but to ignore them and to carry on teaching writing in the ways we have always done would be to significantly disadvantage children. Not only are we in danger of equipping them with a set of skills and knowledge which may already be obsolete, we also risk alienating them by insisting that they ignore the kinds of texts which they see around them and read every day, and produce instead writing to formulae imposed on them from elsewhere.

The examples we give throughout this chapter illustrate how some quite small and subtle changes in classroom practice might begin to acknowledge and address the challenges and issues we outline. Once you start opening up the range of texts that you encourage children to write, sharing and publishing them as widely as you can, you will find that you have set in train a process. This process, in conjunction with the sorts of reading and writing cultures we outline elsewhere in this book, will quickly have an impact on what is written, and how it is written, right across the primary curriculum.

Pictures and words

It is tempting to imagine that many of those exquisite picture story books which we looked at in Chapter 3 came about because the author wrote the story and then asked an illustrator to make her some nice pictures to go with it. This is seldom what happens. More often, if the author and illustrator are not the same person, they result from a careful collaboration between the two, where each revises and refines their work in response to what the other has done. This is not only true of the picture story book: nowadays, in many forms of text it is visual imagery that dominates, words often serving to annotate and clarify. This trend is evident in non-fiction books, newspapers and magazines and, of course, in a whole range of electronic media. In many schools, however, there is still an insistence that the written word must come first and that visual elements, be they drawings or digital pictures, can only come later. For some children it is hugely liberating to be able to represent their ideas graphically before they write. This might be by drawing and/or painting on paper, or perhaps by using some of the wide variety of electronic media that are now widely available in schools – from digital cameras to using drawing and painting software, or even starting by making some digital video or animation. What is important, and what children often understand very well, is that pictures and words work *together* to convey the intended meaning. In his page about motor sport, seven-year-old Ryan has used this understanding to produce work that combines words and visual images to tell his reader all about the sport he loves.

Figure 6.1 Ryan's non-fiction page about motor sport

Changing technology

Many changes in the ways texts look and work are driven by technological innovation. This phenomenon is not new: the novel as a form only became possible once printing and binding could be done relatively cheaply and on a large scale. What does seem to be new is the extraordinary pace at which technological change is now happening, and the way in which new technologies become so widely available so quickly. Digital video is a very good case in point: only a few years ago film and video cameras were far too expensive to have in most schools, too heavy and too fragile to be used freely by children, and the technology for editing was even more expensive and frighteningly complicated to use. Now small digital video cameras and the editing software to accompany them can be bought for little more than the cost of a tank of fuel for a family car and many schools have several available.

These technological changes present us with profound challenges about what we teach and how. It has become all but impossible for teachers to know all about some new technology before they begin to use it with children, and then to teach the children how to use it in an ordered and systematic way. Much more likely, and certainly much more effective, is that they will explore the technology and its possibilities together, learning from each other as they go. This, in turn, can make it very difficult to predict exactly what the outcomes of children's work might look like but, given the space and encouragement to explore and experiment, they are likely to produce results that exceed both our expectations and their own.

Example 1: Making a film of Goldilocks and the Three Bears

These children were a mixed Reception and Year 1 class. They had been working on the story of Goldilocks and the Three Bears. They had heard the story told in a number of versions, read it for themselves, and been offered a number of experiences to encourage them to explore and understand it. Their teacher wanted to offer them another means of telling the story which was as active as possible. They had already done some dramatised retelling of it and the school had just bought some inexpensive digital video cameras. They decided to use these to tell the story.

Anyone who has ever worked with children of this age will know that explaining the technical intricacies of a video camera and the finer points of film grammar will not interest them for long: as soon as they can, they need to be up moving and filming. It took only a few minutes to explain how to use the cameras – they have one button that you press when you want them to film. The teacher just began by asking what the children thought they needed to film first. Their answer was very straightforward: the bears waking up. So off they went into groups to film. Rather than try to teach them all to edit at this early stage, the teacher had the software installed on her interactive whiteboard. With the children, she downloaded each group's clip and the whole class looked at them all, commenting on the similarities and differences. Then they made a plan together about what else needed filming to tell the story. Different groups were allocated different parts of the story to tell and they drew pictures and added a few words to help them remember which parts they were telling and how. There were teaching assistants and other adults who had been brought in for the day to help, so each group was well supported, but the project could also have been undertaken over a number of days with the groups working in turn.

By the afternoon the class were ready to help the teacher assemble their final film. It was a delightful mixture of styles and approaches which none the less told the story clearly, funnily and effectively. Sometimes the bears were played by children, sometimes by teddy bears. But there was no complicated stop-motion animation – when the teddy bears needed to speak, a child talked for them off camera while another jiggled the teddies just enough to give them life. The teacher quickly showed them how to add music and text, and their film was ready to show to the rest of the school.

Of course they were immensely proud of what they had made. Copies were made, put on to CD, and sold to parents. Just as importantly though, these very young children had been challenged to think carefully about the story, its structure and main elements, and the sequence in which it needed to be told. These, of course, are essential skills for the writer.

Example 2: The Home Front

These Year 6 children had been studying Britain since 1930 as part of their history curriculum. They looked particularly at the theme of the Home Front and became interested in the government's public information campaigns of the time. They had looked at posters (*Dig for Victory, Careless Talk Costs Lives, Is Your Journey Really Necessary?*) and also downloaded archive film from the British Pathe site.

Their teacher also showed them a public information film that was made at the outbreak of war. She asked them to watch it in the role of expert film makers, taking careful notes as they did so, and then asked for their professional opinions. Some of them had been asked to attend to particular features such as the music or the spoken commentary. Working from these roles, the children were thoughtfully critical of what they had seen. In her role as the representative from the Ministry of Information, the teacher told the film makers that she wanted to commission them to make more films to be shown in cinemas around the country.

Having accepted the commissions, the children set about researching the campaigns that might be needed. They made posters to be included as stills and titles in their films, wrote scripts and drew storyboards in preparation, and carefully collected all the props and costumes that they thought they would need.

They made their films in groups and, because so much care had gone into the detailed planning and preparation, they were able to work quickly to film and edit. The cameras they used had a very easy-to-use filter that allowed them to turn their films into black and white with a grainy period feel. But the real sense of period of their short public information films came from studying the language and style of the archive footage and reflecting this in the scripts and storyboards they prepared. And, like the other examples we give, their finished products were something in which they could take enormous pride. Not only were they good examples of film making, they also reflected their deep understanding of how film was used at the time, the social and historical background that led to it being used in this way, and how it can still be used persuasively today. Throughout the project they drew and wrote enthusiastically and purposefully, always with that final product in mind.

Possibilities and publication

Not only are new technologies changing the kinds of texts children are able to create, they are also offering many more opportunities to put those texts into the public domain. Publication, in the widest sense of that word, can now be available to all young writers. This may involve using word-processing and desktop publishing software to make books that can be read by other children in the school, but they can also readily publish their work through a website which might make it immediately available to a worldwide audience. Of course there are some issues that surround such publication of which teachers are very well aware, but when the technology is used wisely, it offers means of publication that were unimaginable a generation ago.

Creating not consuming

Many teachers will have entirely understandable anxieties about encouraging children to produce texts that differ widely from those traditionally associated with school. It can certainly feel much safer to be teaching forms of writing that sit neatly on the lines and between the covers of an exercise book, and those forms will continue to have their place. But if we don't encourage children to be active creators of these new and different text forms, then they will only be consumers of them, being done to rather than doing.

Example 3: Moon myths

As part of their reading, this Key Stage 2 class had encountered a Native American myth about the moon and how it came down to earth. They were very taken with the story, particularly a section where Moon is captured by the young men of a village and, in return for his release, agrees to change his face regularly in a way which will help them to mark the changing seasons and know when to sow and when to reap, when to hunt and when to gather. This set the children thinking about why the moon appears to change and some of them researched the phases of the moon. Other children were very interested in other stories that have been told by other cultures about the moon and how it came to be. They researched these stories extensively, using sources from their own library, books borrowed from the local library, and the internet. Another group wanted to know much more about the Apollo space programme of the 1960s and 1970s and conducted similar kinds of research.

Having done all this extensive research and put together an eclectic collection of facts, information, explanations and stories, the children wondered how best to present their work. Rather than leave it all on paper, they decided to create a CD. They quickly recognised that this had a number of advantages. Once made, the CD could be freely copied and everyone could have a copy of everything the class had done; they could also make and sell copies to others, including parents. They recognised that the electronic format would let them put their ideas across in a much wider range of media. As well as including their written work, there were plenty of very high-quality pictures to illustrate it. Those children who had researched other moon myths not only put them on the CD in written form; they also recorded two or three of them so that the reader could click on them and hear the story told as well. Others made drawings to explain the phases of the moon, then scanned these and used simple animation software to bring them to life.

Once they had designed a 'home page' with a large image of the moon in the middle, they added icons of stars around it on which the reader could click to be taken to all the work they had done. As with all such texts, there was no expectation that it should be read in any particular order, and consequently no hierarchy that implied that one form of text or one person's work was any more important than any other.

It is important to stress that this project was undertaken with hardware and software packages that were in school already. The class teacher was not particularly confident in his use of ICT, but sought support from the school's co-ordinator. She, in turn, needed to get help on a couple of points from an LA adviser and the school was also fortunate in having a parent who could offer some extra support with recording sound. When it was finished and shared with the school community, the children and their teacher were immensely proud of what they had made. They can tell you a great deal about the moon too.

Blurring boundaries

When the National Literacy Strategy was introduced in England in 1998, it set out a number of text types and the features of their structure and language use. This type of classification can be very helpful, not only for giving children clear guidance as to what might be expected when they are writing in one of these forms, but also in helping teachers to plan for an appropriate range of reading and writing experience. The particular features of each text type can even be represented diagrammatically to help children understand and remember them. And, particularly if they are going to be publicly tested on their ability to write in these given forms, it is only fair to make sure that children are familiar with them.

In reality of course, the features of different text types and the boundaries between them are much less clear. This is not entirely new: hybrid forms like the fictional diary have been around for centuries. Again though, it is the pace of change that seems unprecedented. And it is not just limited to paper-based media; television documentaries, for example, are now often in a dramatised, semi-fictional form.

Example 4: The ghost of Hamlet's father

These Year 6 children were beginning work on *Hamlet*. Their teacher had used PowerPoint software and a projector to create atmosphere in the hall. She had taken a picture of a castle, used some simple photo-editing software to turn the picture into a ghostly negative that looked like the castle at night, and added some spooky and haunting sounds. The hall was darkened and the children were asked to walk through it as if they were soldiers guarding the castle at Elsinor. As they did so, the teacher narrated that the guards had lately been disturbed on their night watch by what appeared to be the ghost of the late king, Hamlet's father. Staying in their roles as guards, and with the teacher in role as their captain, the children and their teacher improvised a discussion about what they had seen and heard. The conversation quickly focused on whether they should tell the young Hamlet about what had been seen. Having decided that they should, the children were asked to work in pairs to improvise an exchange in which Hamlet is told about his father's ghost. They were introduced to the rhythmic pattern of the iambic pentameter and many of them rose to the challenge of reworking and writing their scene in pentameters, working playfully and imaginatively within the constraint.

Then they were given an extract from the scene in the play where Hamlet first encounters the ghost of his father. It begins:

> Ghost: I am thy father's spirit;
> Doom'd for a certain term to walk the night.

(*Hamlet* Act 1 Sc 5)

The children studied the speech, picking out words and phrases that they found particularly powerful, or of which they merely liked the sound and rhythms. In groups, they used these lines as a stimulus for creating and editing digital photographs. Simple props were used and quickly transformed through the photo-editing process. The flames in the picture below, for example, were made with nothing more than a cardboard box and a pair of scissors.

And for the day confined to fast in fires,
Till the foul crimes done in my days of nature
Are burnt and purged away.

The children also recorded and edited the lines using the simple 'sound recorder' programme that is included with most PCs, adding echoes, repetitions and other effects. The pictures and sounds were combined using PowerPoint and then assembled into a series of slides that were projected to create a speaking image of the ghost, which they used in their later performance of a short version of the play. The use of a free-standing data projector allowed them to project the image high into a corner so that it became further distorted. The ghost was huge and imposing and had a dramatic impact which was reflected not only in the children's performance, but also in the writing that they did as a result. As part of an extended unit of work on the play, the children wrote sections of script, diary entries for some of the characters, and pieces of narrative writing in which they included Shakespeare's lines. They also drew and annotated set and costume designs.

Choosing the right models

It is unsurprising that the emphasis that has been placed on the teaching of literacy in recent years has led to an enormous range of published materials for teachers to use in their classrooms. Often these will contain extracts and examples of the text types which children need to be able to read and write. Their immediate and convenient accessibility clearly makes them very tempting but there is no substitute for collecting as many examples of real texts as you and the children can. Instructions or recipes are very good examples of this: there are plenty published in well-meaning schemes for schools that look like they were written in the 1950s. It is well worth going to the trouble of collecting as many good and current examples as you can, encouraging children and their parents to collect along with you. The range of texts you have available for children should be as wide as possible and, in addition to the rich range of fiction we discussed in Chapter 3, might include:

- A very good-quality, up-to-date non-fiction library which reflects not only your curriculum, but also the major interests of the children.
- Plenty of non-fiction suitable for browsing – a good example would be *Stephen Biesty's Incredible Cross-Sections*, a fabulously illustrated book with which children will happily spend hours and which they will enjoy imitating in their own work.
- Popular non-fiction series such as the *Horrible Histories* by Terry Deary and Martin Browne.
- 'Hybrid' books like *Arthur Spiderwick's Field Guide to the Fantastical World Around You* by Holly Black and Tony DiTerlizzi – this book is presented as a non-fiction 'field guide', but deals with fictional creatures such as the River Troll and the Common House Brownie complete with their Latin names and notes to aid identification. Another one children will love to imitate.
- Books like *Wolves* by Emily Gravett or *The Discovery of Dragons* by Graeme Base, where collections of letters or other non-fiction are used to tell the story.
- A collection of pop-up and lift-the-flap books which children enjoy as models for their own work.
- A good collection of recent comics and graphic novels – these need to be checked regularly to keep them well up to date and remove copies which have become tatty.
- Collections of leaflets and information booklets about the local area and other places that have been/will be visited.
- Collections of instructions, including leaflets, diagrams, DVDs and CD-ROMs.
- Recent magazines and journals, to include children's own interests, lunch-time and after-school clubs and teams, local magazines and newsletters.

Changing patterns of reading

Quite rightly, we encourage children to learn from a very early age that we read text from left to right, from the top of the page to the bottom, and that we finish one page before we turn to the next. For much of the reading that will sustain us for the rest of our lives, this is exactly what we do. But we also know that there have always been types of text that we read very differently. As they get older, we show children how to use an index to find a particular place in a reference book; how to scan the page for the information we need; how to move around the book quickly and efficiently. Lots of contemporary non-fiction books are made to be read and browsed in a non-linear way.

As you open a dramatically and beautifully illustrated double-page spread, it is often difficult to know exactly where to begin and what to read and/or look at first.

Watch someone read a magazine and they will usually start by just flicking through it, pausing occasionally to take a little more in, and then perhaps stopping for a little longer to read an article or feature that is of particular interest. Those bits they passed by the first time they may return to later and some parts of the magazine will stay unread altogether. Electronic forms of media have taken these kinds of reading pattern much further. When was the last time you read the entire contents of a website? Although some sites may have been known to us for some time and others recommended by friends, family or teachers, we chance upon many because of what we choose to type into a search engine. When we reach a site, we might stay and browse for what we find useful or what interests us, but if we can't get what we need we move on pretty quickly. Electronic texts are very seldom composed to be read in any given order and very few have page numbers. Instead, like the 'Moon myths' example, they are likely to have a home page from which we can branch off in whatever direction we need. This wandering, browsing reading is further encouraged by the range of media we may encounter: text, pictures, diagrams, animations, sounds, video, or interactive games. All of these media may combine to inform, entertain or just connect people. And of course a significant and major difference from those written media in the past is the speed at which they can be changed and updated.

Electronic media are often associated with passive behaviour by children and young people – 'sitting for hours in front of a computer screen'. Yet many forms of electronic media also encourage the reader to become a very active participant too. Although they have a very bad name as far as children are concerned, web-based forums where people meet and exchange news and views involve a form of reading that is very immediate and often demands an equally quick response in a written form. Of course we are all too well aware of the dangers of allowing children uncontrolled access, but there is now plenty of software that enables this kind of forum to be established on a school's own intranet, to be accessed only by children in that school, perhaps even only by one class. And they demand a very different kind of reading and writing, also offering very different ways of exploring and discussing issues from the traditional 'hands up in class' discussion.

It is also important to recognise how much new technologies are blurring the boundaries between readers and writers. Web-based encyclopaedias, for example, are not just places where we might go to try to find things out, but also where we are invited to contribute what we know. Opportunities to participate are growing rapidly too.

Changing patterns of writing

When computers, word-processing software and printers first became available in schools, it was not uncommon to see them used only to produce final 'best copies' of children's writing. They were used as rather high-tech typewriters, and only at the very end of the drafting process. Some professional writers still use technology in this way, writing a longhand draft and giving it to someone else to type into a word processor before looking at a proof and making additions, changes and revisions. For others though, the advent of word-processing technology has been extraordinarily liberating. They know that what they write is readily revised, reorganised and corrected. The software will pick up spelling errors and make suggestions about grammar. With layout and font choice made easy, writing can look good from the outset.

For some, these capacities of technology sit uneasily with the need for children to develop legible, fluent and comfortable handwriting; to spell competently and confidently; to construct sentences well at the first attempt; and to set their work out clearly. After all, these skills are still at the heart of current assessment procedures. Of course they remain important, but we also need to recognise that new technologies open up new possibilities for young writers and always have done – otherwise they would still be writing on slates before they were allowed to progress to inkwells and quill pens.

The relative ease with which electronic texts can be revised, corrected and amended has opened up all sorts of new possibilities. This not only applies at the drafting stage; with electronic forms of text it also applies after publication. Good websites are updated, added to and corrected almost by the hour. We no longer need to think and write in a purely linear way; so we can look over what we have done, take note of the ways our audiences have reacted to it, and revise it accordingly. And as we have already pointed out, revisions and additions are not limited to text alone: writers can add pictures, diagrams, sound and video clips at almost any stage in the process. For some young writers it is hugely liberating and motivating.

As we would with any writing, we also need to teach children to use the technology thoughtfully, critically and wisely. Choosing an appropriate font is a very good example. Many young writers – and quite a few older ones too – tend to use the font options as a box of delights from which they can pick and choose, mix and match at will. The results can be ghastly to look at and almost impossible to read. And we have all seen what can happen the first time someone is let lose with a data projector and some presentation software. The resulting cacophony and visual assault as text and images fly from all sides of the screen can be enough to induce seasickness in those expected to endure it. We need to encourage and teach children to make deliberate and thoughtful choices about what they use and how.

Many children, though not all, have access to these technologies at home. Some might even be producing their best work in this way. And many children also carry very sophisticated computer technology with them in the form of their mobile phones. Of course these allow them to do very much more than make phone calls. Few people could have predicted that, given such highly sophisticated technology that will take and send photographs and video clips, children and young people should spend so much of their time writing with them. As well as adding a new verb to the language, texting has generated new forms and conventions of writing which many children understand and use readily. Whatever some older people may think of it, it is a form of writing that is widespread and versatile. We may have quite understandable anxieties about them, but we need to think about how we can make such forms more welcome in the classroom.

Writing together

A great many of the games and strategies that we use throughout this book encourage children to share ideas, to think, plan and write together. Of course it is important that children can also write alone, but writing collaboratively in pairs or groups is also vital. This can range from asking someone else to read work and give an opinion, through to writing which is a genuine collaboration between two or more people. Evolving web-based technologies, and the versions of them that are fast developing for schools, enable and encourage these forms of writing further. There are already plenty of websites where a writer can begin some writing, then invite friends and colleagues to join in.

Taking risks

The examples that we have given all resulted from teachers being prepared to work in an open, exploratory way with their classes. They had ideas about what might be possible, but were not fixed in their expectations of what children might produce. Instead, they encouraged experimentation, drawing the attention of the whole class to what was successful and effective, and challenging the children to push the boundaries further. If this can be the spirit in which we embrace new technologies and the new forms of text they make possible, then we have a genuine chance of engaging, exciting and challenging children with them. Obviously we need to remain critical and keep our expectations high. But the extraordinary range and variety of text types that children can create with such confidence and ease is surely something to be embraced and celebrated.

7 | Practical, productive planning

Nurturing children's writing is a delicate, yet rewarding process requiring patience, imagination and time. When we plan to teach a unit of work, the objectives we set cannot be written in stone; although we might be clear about the type of writing we want them to produce and the skills they will need to engage in the task, we cannot predict at the start of the week what we will expect from our writers by the end. Until we begin, we cannot be sure what support will be needed, what typical mistakes will arise or what will inspire and excite children to write.

If planning seems to have no purpose other than to complete onerous paperwork, it is probably because it is written in too much detail. It may seem like a big risk to hand in a page that carefully outlines the first two days, while the rest of the week contains only a sketchy overview, but to really *teach* writing effectively, your planning needs the space to breathe.

Most effective practitioners work in this way. For them, planning is a tool that helps them to enable learning for children, teachers and teaching assistants. It is less about words in a grid than about thinking and evaluating from the start of the lesson to the end. The changes that these teachers decide in their heads as the lesson goes on are an essential part of the process. By the end of the week their written planning has evolved into a more detailed document, though it certainly doesn't look pristine. It is scribbled on, crossed out and swapped around. Even medium-term plans are annotated in light of the changes. This is planning at its most purposeful.

Planning stands side by side with assessment, recognising where changes need to be made and where more support is required. Really good teaching takes the time to celebrate mistakes because they are something to be learned from. That is why a collection of children's written work is almost like a learning gift for a teacher: a tool that can be used to move children on.

There are some common misconceptions about the Renewed Framework's approach to the immersive writing process. A typical example is that the approach means no writing has to be produced until the end of the week. Some teachers believe that it is now acceptable to do whole days of drama, music, outdoor work and hands-on activity without doing any writing, and that when the end of the week comes, somehow their pupils will remember all the different stimuli and mix them together into a cohesive whole. Of course this should not be the case. If the purpose of all this stimuli is to lead to writing there *has* to be an opportunity for children to capture their ideas along the way. Somehow they have to trap their thoughts on the page, whether they are scribbled, photographed or more carefully crafted. The writing process needs to happen step by step, it cannot just be left to chance. Each time children find words to express something, we need to give them the opportunity to keep hold of it, and usually that means writing it down.

These principles are illustrated with the two studies that follow, one in each Key Stage. The first example (Year 1) outlines an introduction to a unit of work, whereas the second was delivered in the final stages of a unit.

Key Stage 1 case study

Working with Year 1

Under the Sea

It was a real pleasure to work with Sam, a newly qualified teacher who had a passion for teaching writing and was really open to new ideas. There were a few reluctant writers in her class who found it difficult to think of things to write and didn't particularly enjoy putting pen to paper. Not surprisingly, these were the children she really wanted us to target.

The class were working on narrative writing, using the theme of *Under the Sea*. Sam was keen to make this as cross-curricular as possible. The aspect of the writing process in which she wanted support was in providing sensory stimuli to enhance the children's language skills.

The possible outcomes

Through discussion, we realised that *Under the Sea* could lead to all sorts of writing – narrative, poetry and report writing. The sessions we would do with the class would help them to begin to develop exciting language that could apply to different genres.

Sessions 1 and 2

It was important that the children would become fully immersed in the activities, and if they were sufficiently inspired and excited by the work, we would build this motivation as much as possible. So we blocked the first two sessions, making one longer session up to lunch-time.

Year 1 Writing: *Under the Sea*

Sessions 1 and 2 **Outcome** Produce words and phrases that describe the sound of the sea Write questions to send to the sea in the treasure box	Objectives	Activities Step 1	Activity Reflection/Development
	Children practise ways of moving around, in order to stay focused For children to make sea sounds with their voices. This will lead to spelling activities	Children sit on the carpet and look at the treasure chest hidden under the sea scene. Play 'make me a . . .' Stay in a circle. Send the sound of the sea around the circle.	With talking partners, discuss where it has come from and what might be inside it. Explain that the children will need to move around a lot today because they will be exploring the sea. Reflect on the sound that children have made and how quickly it moved around the circle. Discuss the different sounds that the sea can make. Watch an example of the moving sea.
	For children to listen to the sounds they have made and change these into words, either by finding the letter sounds or using descriptive words	Play conductor – children each make their own sounds for the sea. This is then conducted. Different children make sounds at different times. On postit notes, children record as many sounds as they can about the sea and stick them on to the seascape.	Ask children to remember sounds they have made and think of special words to describe them. Children find the secrets of the sea, scattered around the seascape. These are special phrases from the book. They read these in pairs. They are descriptions of the sea from different characters in the story. Children read these out and discuss meanings
	For children to find answers to problems, beginning to create their own narratives	Children then make the sound of the sea and we open up the chest. We look at what is inside (the letter and the book). Focus: 'The Sea knows the answer to many questions and one wave tells another.'	Children make decisions about what should be done with the things we have found in the treasure chest. Start to bank the words in the seascape. Children then write questions to put into the treasure chest to be sent out into the sea.

Figure 7.1 Planning for sessions 1 and 2

Stimuli for writers' voices

Whenever we work with children on a writing project, we need to provide them with something that will provoke thoughts, reactions and opinions.

In this classroom we placed a huge wooden chest in the middle of the carpet area. The chest was covered with sparkly blue, see-through fabrics and we projected a moving image of the sea on to this installation. A recording of the sea played in the background. The children were immediately excited when they walked into the room, straightaway chattering about what they saw.

Objective: For children to start asking questions about what they see

Immediately, the children moved into pairs and talked about:

- where the chest might have come from
- what might be inside it.

It was essential that all pupils felt their responses would be valued. If they said that it was a treasure chest, this was just as good a response as saying that it had come out of somebody's loft or that someone had dumped it in the classroom. By questioning the children further, the stories behind those suggestions started to evolve. Questions like: Who left it? When did they leave it? Why did they think it was a good idea to leave it here? Did they think anyone would find it?

Objective: Children practise ways of moving around in order to stay focused

All the sessions we planned for the children were very active. The learning was going to take place indoors and the space was going to be set up in an unfamiliar way. As we were expecting the children to be excited by what they saw it was important to channel the excitement in a positive way, so we used the 'Make me a . . .' game, outlined in Chapter 2. In silence, the whole class:

*   Found their own space in which to sit around the treasure box.
*   Formed a long straight line in the classroom amongst the tables.
*   Finished up by making a circle.

This brought them on to the next activity, which linked music to writing.

Objective: For children to make sounds of the sea with their voices

First of all, as described in Chapter 5, we taught the children how to send a clap around the circle as quickly as they could. Then they had to send sounds of the sea. We gave them some thinking time before they started, and prompted them to reflect on all the different voices that the sea can have. The result was quite haunting.

Some children waited for the last sound to stop, some layered their responses over the top of the last, and some continued to make their sound all the way through. The responses were wonderful and varied. Because they had heard the sea as they walked in, they were keen to sound out things they had heard with their voices. We also played 'Word orchestra' (see Chapter 5).

Objective: For children to listen to the sounds they have made and change these into words, either by finding the letter sounds or using descriptive words

These fantastic sounds needed to be captured, so we told the children that they could speak back to the sea in its own language. Children moved to tables which had plenty of self-adhesive notes at the ready. On these colourful squares, children recorded the sounds that the sea had made, then stuck them on to the seascape where the treasure chest waited.

They were completely absorbed in this activity. There was no silliness as they moved around to stick their notes in the sea, but lots of gentle noises could be heard as they tuned in to their own voices sounding out the letters they would need. These self-adhesive notes were to be collected up and used as part of the next day's planning.

Objective: For children to find answers to a problem and begin to create their own narratives

So far, all the ideas and language collected in the session had come from the children. Text had not yet been introduced. There was a reason for this: the children needed to know how good their own ideas could be before being shown the parts of the story.

Around the room we had spread lines of text that described the movements and sounds of the sea. This text was taken from different pages of *The Man Whose Mother Was A Pirate* by Margaret Mahy. We asked the children to go and find the lines of text, reading them in pairs. We began by reading a first line, then encouraged children to read their line out when they thought it would best fit in. Sometimes children started reading at the same time, but this didn't matter; if it sounded right they would continue, if it didn't they would wait. We were able to compare ideas from the text to the ideas that children had written on the self-adhesive notes. We talked about the things that the author had written well, and the things that the children had written as well as, or better than, the author.

We wanted the children to be really eager to read the story, so we asked them to surround the chest, make the sound of the sea, and slowly remove the sparkly coverings.

Inside the chest was the book, *The Man Whose Mother Was A Pirate* and a piece of rolled-up parchment, which read:

To whoever finds this letter,

I have run away to be a pirate.

Come and join me so you can learn the secrets of the sea!

At this point, the children moved into pairs. Walking and talking, they discussed what should be done with the letter and the book, then we stopped them and gave them time to respond.

Finally, we selected one of the lines from the story that the children had picked out from the sea to read:

The sea knows the answers to many questions and one wave tells another.

The class formed a circle and whispered questions to each other. Then, on pieces of paper of about A5 size, writing with big, chunky pens, they wrote questions that they would like to ask the sea and put them inside the treasure box. The children had decided that the treasure chest would probably be sent back to the sea, and that some of the questions might be answered.

Main Focus	Assessment and Learning Sheet			
Areas of Learning Covered			Cross Curricular Areas of Learning	

Date:	Learning outcomes:			Comments:
Group:	TARGET			
	1 2 3 4 5			
Group:	TARGET			
	1 2 3 4 5			
Group:	TARGET			
	1 2 3 4 5			

Figure 7.2 Evaluation sheet

Planning for the next session

At the end of the first two sessions, we collected in all of the children's responses and reflected on their progress. We used the tick sheet (see Figure 7.2), writing the names of the children down the side, organised in ability groupings. Though the children did not necessarily work in this way, this meant we were still able to ensure that all levels of ability were appropriately challenged. The tick sheet took less than five minutes to complete, and using a scale of 1 to 5 – where 1 was underachieving and 5 was exceeding expectations – it was possible to consider how well each child had progressed in the lesson. Both teaching assistants and teachers completed the same sheet, carefully considering the children they had worked with. It was a very quick way of focusing the direction of the learning for the next lesson.

After gathering the children's responses and ideas, certain aspects of the planning needed to be adapted. A focus for the next lesson would be based on one of the children's own questions: Does the sea have feelings? This would lead in to some work on personification.

We had noticed that by using a musical activity to inspire the children's responses, they were able to describe the sea in surprisingly original ways. One child (who had actually made a purr sound) wrote that the 'sea purred'; another made up her own special words, 'the sea says tish tash'.

Session 3

Year 1 Writing: *Under the Sea*

Session 3	Objectives	Activities Step 1	Activity Reflection/Development
Outcome Produce group jottings using words that personify the sea	Revise and build on work from previous sessions	Explain that the chest has gone back into the sea and we are going to write a poem about the sea.	Introduce one of the children's questions. 'Does the sea have feelings?'
	For children to connect sounds and senses to writing	Children form a circle. Give out words for them to read. The words are a combination of those they wrote down yesterday and words from the book.	Children think about how their word might be said. They group themselves within the circle depending on the strength of the word. Play conductor, making the sound of the sea once more.
	To use a stimulus to inspire ideas about the sea. Linking visual images to their work	Return to the question: 'Does the sea have feelings?' Play feelings game. Write synonyms on the board as children guess the feeling.	Show moving image of the sea. Children decide how the sea may be feeling in this shot. We discuss other possibilities and link feelings to sounds.
	To suggest a frame to guide children in their writing, allowing them to draw on the words and images they have created over the last three sessions	Model writing some poetic phrases about the sea: When the sea is feeling… It…..and it….. It….., ……. And ………	Children use their collections of words and phrases to prompt them in their writing.

Figure 7.3 Planning for session 3

Objective: Revise and build on work from previous sessions

We discussed some of the imaginative questions that children had placed in the treasure chest. There were wonderful ideas: Are you alive or are you dead? Where is your brain? Where is your heart? Do you have feelings? In a circle we walked around the chest and thought about possible answers. One boy said that the sea's brain was right on the top of the waves where it was white and frothy, another child said that the sea was a ghost because you could see through it.

The main focus for the lesson was going to be whether the sea had feelings. We wanted to celebrate some of the responses children had used when they had written sounds of the sea on self-adhesive notes. We had typed out all the responses and given them back to the children, so they looked just as important as the words from the book. Examples included:

The sea whispers

The sea moans

The sea growls

The sea groans

The sea roars

Sshhhh

Crrrr

The sea creaks

The sea trembles

The sea is like white horses neighing

Objective: For children to connect sounds and senses to writing

We played 'Word orchestra' in the circle once more; this time, when I pointed to the children, they read out the phrase they were holding in their hand, using a voice that sounded like the character of the sea.

Objectives: To use a stimulus to inspire children to think imaginatively about the sea; To enable children to link visual images to their work

The next step was to show the children different video clips of the sea. We made sure that the clips were contrasting, showing the sea at its liveliest and at its most gentle.

As the children watched, we asked them to think about the character that the sea was displaying in each clip. In order to extend their language skills, we played the game 'In the manner of the word'. One person goes out of the room, while those remaining think of a word that describes a feeling. Re-entering the room, the 'guesser' prompts the children to do something, but they must do it in the manner of the word. The first time we played this, the chosen word was 'angry'. The child who returned to the room asked them to read their books in this way, so they acted out being angry readers.

Objective: To suggest a frame to guide children in their writing, allowing them to draw on the words and images they have created over the last three sessions

After reading more of the story, and collecting some of the language we really liked, we modelled writing a poem that described the sea's moods. Because the focus was on using the language and using personification, we gave the children a structure to hook on to. The underlined words show the joining phrases that we offered the children that would help to link their ideas together.

> When the sea is sleepy
> It purrs and it yawns
> It spreads out its broad blue back and sighs.

Children of all abilities worked really well at this, the more able being encouraged to push out of the suggested frame if they wanted to.

Planning for the final sessions

As this was the first step of the narrative writing project which the teacher was going to take three weeks to cover, we decided that in the final sessions we would do some more

Sessions 4 and 5	Year 1 Writing: *Under the Sea*		
Outcome	**Objectives**	**Activities Step 1**	**Activity Reflection/Development**
Create graphic musical notation	Use sensory approaches to stimulate children's thinking	The room is changed around so the children sit on the carpet around the treasure chest. The sound of the sea is played in the background and moving images of the sea are projected on to the chest.	Discuss what might be in the chest. Listen to the sound of the sea. Ask children what the sea is saying to us?
Connect words to notation	Produce a thought shower in groups	Power of the pen: Children write down all the words they can think of to describe how they are feeling about the treasure chest. They then write down all the sentences they can, telling us what the sea will say if we take the treasure chest.	We think back to the original appearance of the treasure chest, the letter and the book. We read the next part of the story.
	Imagine part of the narrative	Children go back to the circle. They turn their backs to the chest and think of something that may be inside. When tapped on the shoulder, they call out what is inside.	As a class we think of a chant to call out. When we stop the chant, the children call out the many voices of the sea.
		We move closer to the chest and carefully remove the coverings. Then we shake the chest, and carefully open it up.	Talk about where the instruments come from.
	Practise control when using instruments	Pass the shell hat and bells around the circle in different directions – in absolute silence.	Model graphic notation. Children interpret the shapes with their voices.
		Give out instruments. Children make three soft sounds with them.	Play conductor.
	Link sounds to images	Children write own graphic notation to go with their sound.	Children write words next to their symbols, reflecting sounds and thoughts of the sea.
		Read the end of the story.	

Figure 7.4 Planning sessions 4 and 5

work to draw out the language and we wanted to continue to explore the narrative that had been developed with the children. What would happen when the chest returned from the sea? What would it contain? The children had responded so well to the musical stimulus that we decided to extend this further by using musical instruments and encouraging the children to work with graphic notation.

Year 6 case study

World War II evacuees

Possible writing outcome: To write a report which presents a realistic view of evacuation in World War II.

Tracey is an experienced practitioner who constantly adapts her planning to meet the needs of the children. The challenge she had working with her new class was that they did not seem to think very deeply about things. When given a question or provocation, they didn't dig far under the surface to respond to it. They would tend to answer with the first thing that occurred to them, rather than being reflective. She wanted to make the work cross-curricular and was keen to move beyond the fascination that Year 6 boys sometimes have with bombing and blood. So we decided to focus on evacuees.

Short Term Planning Year 6 Autumn Term		Report Writing Based on World War II Evacuees

Learning Outcome Use the styles and conventions of journalism to create a voice over for modern documentary about World War II
Objectives Over the Unit: *linked to note taking*
1. (S) Use the techniques of dialogic talk to explore ideas, issues or topics 2. (L+R) Make notes throughout the session, capturing language, ideas and reflections 4. (D) Improvise with tableaux and in role to explore the mixed feelings connected with evacuation 6. (WS+Sp) Employ a range of strategies to spell difficult and unfamiliar words Use a range of appropriate strategies to edit, proofread and correct own work 7. (U+I) Appraise Film, newspaper article, personal account and photographs recognise persuasive devices 8. (E+R) Consider the different ways in which evacuation has been presented by different people at different times 9. (C+ST) Integrate words with film 12. (P) Communicate ideas using ICT

(Numbered Objectives based on those in Renewed Framework for Literacy)

Voice Finding Stimuli: Image projection, Film, Photographs, Newspaper Report, Account from Evacuee, Alone on a Wide Wide Sea, Recording of Princess Elizabeth. Exploration through drama

Step	Broken Down Objectives leading to Outcome	Activity	Further Activity/Reflection
		M O N D A Y	
	Outcome: To have recorded a short personal phrase about being evacuated. To have jotted down useful words and phrases. To have appraised an image and piece of text, thinking carefully about the message behind it and whether it is a reliable source.		
1	To challenge children to look beneath the surface	Project image of Evacuees arriving at the station into the corner of the room. Children to use 'paper magnifying glasses', catching the image in their hands *We spent more time on this activity in order to deepen children's thinking skills*	In pairs, children shower down as many things they have noticed as possible in writers' notebooks. Whole class activity, mixed ability. Children are told not to worry about spellings, no idea is too silly, simple ideas lead to great ideas and quantity is important *To draw out better ideas we reflected on this as a whole class*
③ ②	After watching a newsreel showing evacuees leaving for Australia, to pick out the language used, and discuss whether this is a reliable source *To notice subtle detail and pick up on the power of suggestion*	Children watch film clip twice. The first time watch then discuss I pairs, the second time calling out language that stands out. *Drama Tableaux → for steps. In the home. On the way to the station. At the ... on their own*	Two minutes to shower down memorable phrases on large pieces of flip chart. Same rules as above, but sitting in ability groupings. *Whole class response + what does body language tell us?*
3	To compare the newsreel to a newspaper report. Pick out similarities and differences, highlight the language used and discuss how reliable it is as a source *Leave until tomorrow*	Children work in pairs, highlighting with highlighter pens.	After it has been modelled on the board, jot down similarities and differences on A3 paper to be added to working wall.
4	To consider the differences between children's reactions on and off camera. Discuss why this might be different. *To develop empathy*	Children move into groups of 3, walking in a circle around the chair which symbolises the camera *Children walk around in a circle imagining they are walking to the station.*	Pick up on children's body language, discuss what they are carrying in their bags. Children to write down a sentence about themselves on a post it, to stick onto photograph on working wall

Figure 7.5 Year 6 planning sessions 1 and 2

We thought that the best way to challenge the thinking in Year 6 was to look at some newsreels and posters that were produced to encourage parents to send their children away. Eventually we wanted them to do a voice-over report that would look back at the events with a contemporary, perhaps less one-sided view of events. As this report would be for a television-type documentary, we might need to use emotive language to touch the hearts of the viewer.

Session 1

Objective: To challenge children to look beneath the surface

We projected a detailed image of evacuees arriving at a station which flooded into the corner of the room. Because it was not shining on to a flat surface, the image was unclear so the children had to explore it in a different way (as outlined in Chapter 5). Working in pairs, numbered one or two, children explored the image, letting it spill on to blank A4 paper which they held up to the light. Number ones moved in first, allowing number twos to stand back and observe. There was an audible gasp from the children as the image appeared. Watching the effect of the image spilling on to hands, bodies and paper was spellbinding.

After two minutes, the children rejoined their partners and jotted down all they could remember. Their initial responses were quite disappointing: 'Evacuees . . . gas masks . . . children . . . station . . .'. So when we asked the number twos to step into the picture we had to challenge them to look for clues about how the people in the picture might be feeling.

When they came out of the picture, again the responses were rather limited: 'smiling . . . happy . . . laughing'. It was clear that so far, the children were only commenting on what they saw on the surface. They would need approaches that would challenge this in the next day's planning and we would have to adjust what we were doing that day.

We asked the children to step to the side as we held up a large piece of paper to catch one image in the centre of the picture – that of the station master. First, they viewed his whole face, which they observed was happy and smiling. Then we showed just his eyes. We allowed the children to chat in pairs for a minute about what they thought they were seeing. Now the children were beginning to think:

> His eyes make him look tired and old . . . they are focused on a child but they are not really looking at them . . . they seem to be full of sadness . . . they seem quite distant.

This opened up an interesting discussion about why the station master was trying to smile, when inside he might feel sad. Then the children looked at the picture again. Again, their responses were much more considered. They found, 'tiny hands gripping tightly to other hands . . . a little boy dressed up like a dad . . . highly polished shoes . . . small bags hanging from shoulders . . . children looking lost'.

At this point, without reading any text, they were beginning to think about the deeper issues surrounding World War II evacuation and starting to think more like writers.

Adapting the objective: To develop empathy

We believed that we were about to reach a turning point with the class so we needed to press on. Rather than moving straight on to text and film as originally planned, we decided to stretch their thinking further through drama. We hoped that Year 6 might physically sense how the evacuees might be feeling by thinking about the scene in the home of an evacuee, moments before they had to leave.

Children moved into groups of four or five and were asked to make four freeze frames (tableaux):

- A moment in their house.
- The moment they walked out of their front door.
- The moment when they said goodbye to their parents.
- The moment when they could no longer see each other.

Through this drama strategy we were able to track the transition of feelings. Picking out the example of one group, we were able to stand back and look at the way their bodies behaved, as if looking into a picture. At this stage we needed to prompt the class: 'describe their body language . . . what does it tell us?' Now children were starting to identify things like: 'their eyes are looking down . . . their shoulders are hung low . . . the mum is standing up very straight and tall and she is smiling. She has her hand on her child's shoulder.'

The children noticed that, 'as the children move closer to the station, their body language changes. They start to stand taller and look braver as they see more children.'

And, 'When the mum can't see her children anymore, her body language changes completely. Immediately her shoulders slump and she starts to cry.'

Objective: To consider the reasons why so many parents agreed to evacuate their children

We then showed children a short film that we had downloaded from British Pathe, the sort that would have been shown in cinema newsreels. As the children watched, we encouraged them to call back any language that really stood out for them. This included words and phrases such as 'chins up' and 'adventure'.

After watching and calling, we gave them a minute to record as many responses as they could remember. They showered these words down with chunky pens on pieces of flip chart paper that covered the desk. Every child in the class had to write something. This allowed them to capture words that might be useful to them in their later writing. It also led into a detailed discussion about the reasons parents felt obliged to send their children away. This would be picked up further in another lesson.

Objective: For children to imagine that they are an evacuee, writing a phrase to describe how they might have felt

We had not planned to finish the lesson in this way, but the children had moved on so far in the space of one lesson that they needed to own and capture the experience.

Again we projected the image into the corner of the room and played a different film of evacuation (also available from British Pathe), this one having a voice-over from the young Princess Elizabeth who was sending a personal message to all the children who were moving away from 'their mummies and daddies'. Children moved around the room in a circle, imagining they were walking on the station platform. We asked them to think of a phrase that would either describe how they were feeling, or tell us about something they were carrying with them. When Princess Elizabeth finished her message, we asked the children to record their responses on self-adhesive notes. They did this readily. Tracey, the class teacher, was particularly pleased with a boy who had very little confidence in his writing ability and didn't usually write much down. He filled two labels, writing in tiny handwriting to get down as much detail as he could. He wrote:

> Shocked and worried, I carry pictures, my football, my teddy bear.
> My shoulders hang low, I'm concentrating on the ground and inside, I feel sick.
> Tightly, I hold my sister's hand.

Because we used small squares of colourful paper, he did not feel anxious about having to fill a large blank space with words. The fact that he could then hold those small squares in his hand meant that the writing was more personal. Another child that stood out was a boy with autism, who was said to 'hate literacy'. Throughout the session, his responses had been some of the most original, but the final phrase that he recorded was very interesting:

> I wonder whether everyone else is hurting inside, if they too, want to stay. I wonder whether we will ever see our families again.

His involvement in the drama had really helped him to empathise with the evacuees because he had experienced it himself through enacting it.

Planning for the next session

In just one lesson, the whole class had moved on a long way. They had become more analytical, and were beginning to use suggestion to describe feelings, rather than obvious

I wonder whether everone else is hurting inside, if they too, want to stay. I wonder whether we will ever see our families again.

My tummy is tight, my hands are gripped. My eyes are looking at the ground.

Butterflies rise in my tummy.

Shocked and worried **(bewildered?)**, I carry pictures, my football, my teddy bear.

My shoulders hang low, I'm concentrating on the ground and inside, I feel sick.

Tightly, I hold my sister's hand.

My angry body is nauseous, my stomach is churning.

Head stuffed with memories.

Eyes are wet with sorrow.

My eyes are tearful but my mouth is trying to smile.

Quaking legs.

Quivering hands, stomach pulled tight.

My whole body is shaking, as I grasp onto my teddy.

Head bowed down, remembering the memories of my family, this is what I take.

Clutching my little sister's hand, I flick the pages of my scrapbook, shuffling nervously, tearfully in my seat.

I take a photograph of my mum and dad and family, clasping that photograph tightly.

Figure 7.6 The children's phrases

phrases such as 'they were nervous', or 'they looked happy but were sad'. The phrases the children had recorded needed to be valued so they were typed up ready to share and discuss.

Session 2

Objective: To celebrate the strong points in children's writing

We gave out the typed out examples of writing and asked pupils to work in pairs. They had two minutes to read the sheets and think about all the things that were good about the work. Then they had one minute to shower down as many positive comments as they could think of on the back of the sheet. There was a strong celebratory atmosphere in the room, which fired pupils up to be ambitious in their writing.

Objective: To get better at noticing things beneath the surface

Spread out around the room were 28 different pictures of children in World War II settings (a quick image search on the internet will find plenty). Children moved in and out of them, until they were counted down, 5, 4, 3, 2, 1. At 1, the children had to stop at a picture, turn it over and look at it for one minute. After that, they were given a further minute to jot down as many ideas as they could.

Short Term Planning Year 6 Autumn Term			Report Writing Based on World War II Evacuees	
Learning Outcome: Use the styles and conventions of journalism to create a voice over for modern documentary about World War II Objectives Over the Unit:				
1. (S) Use the techniques of dialogic talk to explore ideas, issues or topics 2. (L+R) Make notes throughout the session, capturing language, ideas and reflections 4.(D) Improvise with tableaux and in role to explore the mixed feelings connected with evacuation 6.(WS+Sp) Employ a range of strategies to spell difficult and unfamiliar words, Use a range of appropriate strategies to edit, proofread and correct own work 7. (U+I) Appraise Film, newspaper article, personal account and photographs, recognise persuasive devices 8. (E+R)Consider the different ways in which evacuation has been presented by different people at different times 9. (C+ST) Integrate words with film 12. (P) Communicate Ideas using ICT				
(Numbered Objectives based on those in Renewed Framework for Literacy)				
Voice Finding Stimuli: Image projection, Film, Photographs, Newspaper Report, Account from Evacuee, Alone on a Wide Wide Sea, Recording of Princess Elizabeth, Exploration through drama				
Step	Broken Down Objectives leading to Outcome		Activity	Further Activity/Reflection
TUESDAY: DOUBLE SESSION UP TO LUNCHTIME				
Outcome: To have started the introduction of a report for the a modern television documentary that wishes to attract an audience				
1	To celebrate strong points in children's writing	Give out typed out examples of writing face down. Children move into pairs. They have 2 minutes to read the sheets and remember as many positive points as possible about the work.	Children turn over the sheets and have 2 minutes to record as many positive points as they can think of. Same rules as yesterday – no judgement etc.	
2	To get better at noticing things beneath the surface	Photographs depicting children in World War II laid out, face down around the room. Children move in and out of them, until they are counted down to stop at one. They turn it over, and observe it for one minute.	Mixed ability groupings • Children turn the sheets over and record as many things as they can about what they have seen on the back of the picture • Children move around again, this time stopping at a different image. First they read the points already made, then look at the picture, finding new things to say. Teacher models a good example to help them know what to look for. Layered Expectations – a) What the picture tells us about setting, feelings, motivation b) What the picture tells us about setting c) Picking up on more subtle details	
3	Return to the films and consider whether they offer a realistic depiction of World War II evacuation. Compare this to a newspaper article	Discuss type of language used in film clip for evacuation. Was it right to offer this view in such troubled times? Why was this the case? Use highlighter pens to pick out key phases in newspaper reports that could be challenged.	Paired Discussion, Walk and Talk, leading to Whole class discussion Refer back to history lesson. What is known about the reality of evacuation? When highlighting work, expectations: a) Pick out phrases that could be challenged by evidence b) Pick out phrases that could be challenged and say why c) Pick out key phrases that could be challenged	
4	After observing a report being written, write an introduction using strong words and phrases that have been developed throughout the sessions	Children to watch mistakes being made and changed as the introduction is modelled. They observe carefully how key phrases are used in the text for meaning, clarity and effect. Children are reminded of places where they can refer to good language – notebooks, working wall, text, flip-charts, typed out examples	Children (working in pairs if they wish) write the introduction. Expectations a) Write in the style of a television report, using emotive language and following the structure modelled. Proof read work and consider where how the work might progress – without support a) Write in the style of a television report, using emotive language and following the structure modelled – without support c) Children write report supported by T	

Figure 7.7 Year 6 planning session 2

Just as we had in the previous lesson, we really wanted to extend the children's thinking. It would no longer be good enough for them merely to record the obvious things. This time, they would move around again, ending up at a new picture where they would need to read the comments that had already been written down. After this they would have a further minute to write down extra things they had noticed. Responses were improving all the time. One child noticed a 'worn out bible on a bedside table', another child wrote, 'you can tell it is winter because they are wearing jackets made of fur'.

Objectives: Return to the films and consider whether they offer a realistic depiction of World War II evacuation; Compare this to a newspaper article

After watching the film clips again, we discussed the positive language that was used to persuade people of the merits of evacuation. We considered whether it was morally right to offer such a one-dimensional view of the picture in troubling times. Children were able to refer back to the information they were starting to gather in their history lessons about how difficult life was for many evacuees. We wondered how British newspapers depicted the event.

Objective: To model writing a newspaper report, using strong words and phrases that have been developed throughout the sessions

After reading a newspaper report from the time (we used coverage from the *Daily Mirror* which was available on the internet), children annotated phrases that they wanted to challenge such as 'smiling and cheerful', 'no hitch', and 'great adventure'. We then thought about how different the article might look if it were more realistic. Everyone agreed that they would like to use many of the ideas they had developed over the course of the two sessions.

Modelling how to write the report was going to be essential because the children needed to see the process that writers work through when getting their ideas on paper. They needed to see that first ideas don't have to be perfect. We started with the introduction:

> Evacuation of school children from London may have run smoothly, but it was with heavy hearts that mothers left the station.
>
> 'I just hope that I've done the right thing and that they won't be away too long', one mother confided. She was clutching a little teddy bear that her child had given to her as a goodbye present.
>
> When asked what she had taken with her, one evacuee replied, 'I haven't taken much but my head is stuffed with memories'.

As the writing was modelled we used as many examples of the children's words and phrases as we could:

> Another child, whose eyes were wet with sorrow clutched tightly onto their little sister's hand saying, 'Come on, we are going on an adventure . . .'.

As we wrote out this introduction we purposely made mistakes, crossing out words and making changes for the children to see. After watching this process, the children were ready to write an introduction themselves. They had the structure of the article as a hook, and a wealth of words and phrases they could refer to and use in their writing.

Children were encouraged to work in pairs if they wanted to. The atmosphere was very productive and the children were proud of their work.

Session 3

Objective: (Main) To learn what to look for when improving writing; To spell polysyllabic words

This lesson began with a quick spelling game which we call 'Word beat'. Children listened to polysyllabic words, worked out the number of syllables and then drew a dash for each beat. For example, the word 'important' would look like this: _ / _ / _.

Short Term Planning Year 6 Autumn Term		Report Writing Based on World War II Evacuees	

Learning Outcome: Use the styles and conventions of journalism to create a voice over for modern documentary about World War II
Objectives Over the Unit:
    1. (S) Use the techniques of dialogic talk to explore ideas, issues or topics 2. (L+R) Make notes throughout the session, capturing language, ideas and reflections 4.(D) Improvise
    with tableaux and in role to explore the mixed feelings connected with evacuation 6.(WS+Sp) Employ a range of strategies to spell difficult and unfamiliar words, Use a range of
    appropriate strategies to edit, proofread and correct own work 7. (U+I) Appraise Film, newspaper article, personal account and photographs, recognise persuasive devices 8.
    (E+R)Consider the different ways in which evacuation has been presented by different people at different times 9. (C+ST) Integrate words with film 12. (P) Communicate Ideas
    using ICT
 	
    (Numbered Objectives based on those in Renewed Framework for Literacy)			

Voice Finding Stimuli: Image projection, Film, Photographs, Newspaper Report, Account from Evacuee, Alone on a Wide Wide Sea, Recording of Princess Elizabeth, Exploration through drama			
Step	Broken Down Objectives leading to Outcome	Activity	Further Activity/Reflection
WEDNESDAY			
Outcome: To have proofread own work, making adjustments and improvements. To have written the main body of the report.			
1	To learn what to look for when improving writing: Spelling	Revise polysyllabic words. – Play games Play 'Teacher These'	Play 'Word Beat' in pairs (spelling adapted for ability grps) Revise rules there, their, they're / plurals double cons
2	To learn to proof read for meaning and effect	Play 'Carousel Critic.' Respond on adhesive notes. Use examples of typical mistakes in writing. Notes	Picking up on commonalities – changing tenses – making text personal – exaggeration/inappr use of plurals/vocab
3	To improve own work and to write the next part of the report	Children watch modelling of next section. Discuss how to read marking comments	Children write next section. Bs) More input from Teacher - picking up on typical ind questions As) indeptly – more support tomorrow Cs) Independetly with frame as guide
4	To evaluate learning from lesson .	Quick return to spellings – how many do you know now on list Discuss changes children are proud of	Fold over paper Try those you can do Discuss things that children would change next time

※   * Play 'Call Back' Listening to extract
             from 'Alone on a wide wide sea.

Figure 7.8 Planning for session 3

The children could tick each syllable that was correctly spelt. We then moved on to looking at typical spelling mistakes that the class had made in their own writing:

there (belonging to)
diserbance
everythink
apperered
familys
noing
destroued
steped
unknowen
cluching

After being invited to 'teacher these . . .' – a phrase they like to use to indicate that they are in the role of corrector and teacher – children worked in pairs to correct as many as they could in a time limit of four minutes. Afterwards we went through each word, talking about rules and useful ways to remember them, learning a rhyme to remember how to spell 'there', 'their' and 'they're'. We were to return to the spellings at the end of the lesson.

Objective: To learn to proofread writing for meaning and effect

It was essential that we also considered the structure and style of the writing itself. Again, there were common mistakes. We wanted to discuss these in a positive way, while giving children the ownership and motivation to make improvements.

We explained that we had written out sentences in our own words, but that the examples contained the sorts of mistakes that more than one person had made in the class.

Carefully differentiating the tasks for ability groups, we played 'Carousel critics'. Children sat in groups of six, and had to work in pairs. Each pair had a different piece of writing to look at. They had two minutes to jot down on self-adhesive notes as many points as they could think of to move the writer on. These comments could be celebratory or examples of constructive criticism. After this, they 'carouselled' their sheet to the next pair and received a new one. This time they had only a minute to respond. The final time, they had only 30 seconds to respond. These are some of their corrections and comments:

The sentence 'You could see their quaking legs and churning stomachs' got the comments:

- You have used powerful language.
- Can you see someone's stomach churning?
- You have used the word 'you' and you are writing a report.

For 'With tearstains on their face, they got on the train ready for a journey to their worst nightmare' they commented:

- Face should have an s.
- You have used good language and said about people's actions.
- How did they know it was going to be their worst nightmare?

And 'The railway officials were not used to seeing so many children on a train without adults. Looks like they're just going now!' got:

- You have changed tenses.
- You have made it sound like you are talking at the end.

This was followed by a whole-class feedback session.

Without having their own work scrutinised in front of others, children were able to recognise the mistakes that they had made in their writing and were keen to put them right. This was a positive, collaborative exercise, so children did not feel downhearted about redrafting their writing. Rather, they felt enthused to make the changes themselves.

Objective: To improve own work and to write the next part of the report

The children watched as we modelled the next section of text. Then they had time to look at comments, make improvements, ask individual questions and continue with their writing. All the work had been carefully marked, with constructive comments and points for improvement, so individuals were clear about expectations.

Objective: To evaluate how much we have learned in the lesson

Picking out some of the polysyllabic words in the list of spelling mistakes, children played 'Word beat' once more. Using this strategy, the whole class were able to spell, for example, the word 'disturbance'. Children were also invited to be brave and show where they had made changes they were proud of in their writing. One girl had used a thesaurus to look up the word 'brave' and had tentatively written the words 'courageous/audacious' above it. After being prompted to look up the term in the dictionary, she had made the decision that although 'audacious' sounded a really impressive word, 'courageous' was far closer to the feeling she was trying to express.

Session 4

Objective: To ask searching questions

For this session we started in the hall, where six different photographs were given out to the class. Each pair sat behind a picture, with self-adhesive notes at the ready. The challenge was to look at the picture and think of as many questions as possible that they would like to ask, writing one question per label and 'dumping' them on the picture. This would then become part of the class interactive display and be the basis of some of the learning they would cover in their history topic.

This activity really showed how far the children's thinking had progressed. One boy had been studying a picture of four smiling children with their trousers rolled up standing in a lake. He said:

> I'd like to know who was taking the photograph and why. Their smiles look a bit weird. They don't look like they're really happy. They look a bit cold in that water, their bodies look a bit stiff.

Objective: To use writing as a voice-over for a modern-day documentary about World War II evacuation

As a final activity, the group moved into the computer suite, where they were able to download and watch the films. Working in pairs, trying out their work one at a time, they read their words over the top of the moving films. They were given the opportunity to add ideas, change words, or expand on certain details. Using the film and relating it to the written word made this a very powerful editing process.

Creating Writers in the Primary Classroom

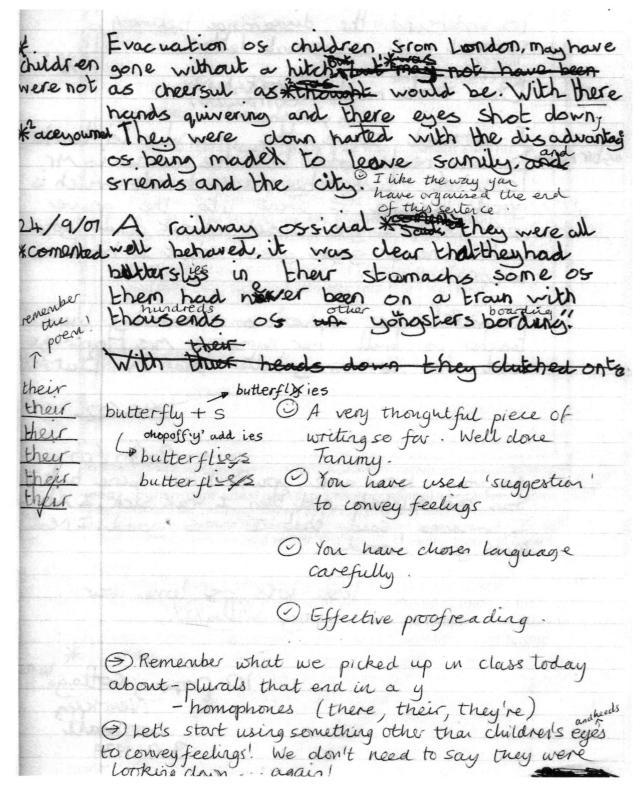

Figure 7.9 Tammy's work in progress

110

The class teacher was particularly pleased with one boy, who she knew had ability but had not been performing well up to this point. His finished writing was very impressive.

Evacuation of children from London may have gone without a hitch, but behind some of the smiles, sorrow and shock cowered.

Reluctantly, each child clutched a gas mask, along with their treasured possessions.

'We have been herded and ushered to unknown destinations,' noted a tearful evacuee.

Strong wills were aplenty as the young explorers marched in unison to the halls and schools to acquire their 'new families'. Nervously, each child pondered what sort of family they might have.

Back at home, mothers tried their best to believe the words on public announcements and posters.

'Your children will be safe!'

Although there is much that could still be improved in this writing, it is none the less compelling and it is clear that the writer believed in what he was writing and wanted to truly engage the reader.

In both case studies, good-quality writing was the result of a carefully considered process which included plenty of opportunities for children to be active in their learning. Planning and objectives were adapted for the pupils so they could recognise every day how their learning needs had been taken into account.

When their writing needed to be improved, they never lost ownership of their work and, in both examples, writing was not just an independent activity to be completed at a desk, it was something to be shared and celebrated with others. Sometimes the writing was as big as the table, sometimes as small as a label, but however big or small its beginnings, the finished work was something that mattered a great deal to children and teachers alike. They were writing together and writing well.

8 | Building a community of writers

In Chapter 3 we stressed the importance of good books in developing young writers and explored some of the ways in which schools can develop a 'reading culture': one where books and other forms of writing are read, shared, enjoyed and celebrated by everyone in and around the school. When you walk into a 'reading school' the signs are usually there from the start. High-quality literature is everywhere; thoughtfully displayed and supported by a range of exciting stimuli. That range includes posters, some commercially produced and some made by children, displays about a particular book or series which might include artefacts, toys or puppets, story tapes, videos and DVDs. There are plenty of books and other literature for everyone to browse as they wait in a reception area, and as you walk around the school the interest and excitement hits you everywhere you look. In such a school, when you start talking to children about books you know you are going to be there for some time as they chat readily and confidently about what they read and enjoy. Perhaps the most significant characteristic of all is that children regard themselves as readers in the fullest sense.

Very many teachers will recognise this description of a 'reading school'; it may be just the kind of school you are lucky enough to work in every day. But how might we recognise a 'writing school'? What practical steps can we take to build a similar culture of writing?

Start at the beginning

The four-year-old children who were working in the florist's shop that we describe in Chapter 4 took writing in their stride and accepted it as a natural and necessary part of their life and work in the shop. When the adult who was role playing the van driver asked for directions to be written down, the children did so willingly and confidently. Keeping that spirit alive is one of the biggest challenges we face, not least because the kind of confident mark making that typifies their work in the shop has at some point to embrace the skills, rules and formal conventions of writing. It is all too easy for children to experience a very sudden jolt: from feeling confident that their playful marks are accepted and welcomed by the adults around them, to a sense that writing is something that they cannot yet do and that it will be a mighty hard slog to learn.

Good early years practice provides the foundation on which the writing school builds. The classrooms are rich with spoken and written language. Teachers listen to children, value the experiences and interests they bring to school, encourage them to ask questions and play with ideas. Opportunities to write and draw are everywhere. There is a plentiful supply of paper of different sizes, texture and quality. They are encouraged to experiment with all sorts of ways of writing: not only are there plenty of crayons, pens and pencils, but also typewriters and computers, chalks for writing huge letters on the playground, sand trays for feeling the shapes of letters, and plenty of paint. They experiment with writing in the dirt, with making giant letters from stones and pebbles so they might be rescued from the island they have created in their role play, and they write each other codes and secret messages. In the writing school, everyone has learned from this practice and all the classrooms are well and thoughtfully resourced 'writing classrooms'.

Resources for the writing classroom

Building a community of writers in the primary school begins in the classrooms. Not only are the best classrooms places where children learn to construct sentences, punctuate and spell; they are also places which profoundly affect attitudes to writing and give children an enduring sense that it is something they can do and enjoy. The resources in the room have a significant impact on those attitudes and how they develop through a child's time in school. The following list is far from exhaustive, but it offers a starting point from which you might review your own classroom.

A good range of writing implements

Most of us recognise the frustration that comes with trying to use a ball-point pen that is running out or a pencil that is too short to hold comfortably and keeps breaking. For inexperienced writers that frustration can be even greater. All that we offer needs to be in good condition, easy and comfortable to use. We need a good range from the large felt-tip pens that we might use when we are collecting ideas in groups, through the crayons and coloured pencils that we use for a wide range of texts, to good-quality pens and pencils that children have to hand all the time. In the writing classroom, not having a pen or pencil is never used as a reason not to write. Computers also form part of this range: sometimes using them throughout the writing process; sometimes at specific stages in it. Ideally, printers will be easily accessible and well maintained, but children also need to learn to use them sensibly and economically.

A good range of paper – types and sizes

As we have illustrated throughout, there may be many stages in the development of a finished piece of writing. Each stage may require a different type of paper – from the scraps that might be used to generate initial ideas, to self-adhesive notes for planning and organising, to plain paper for drawing storyboards, maps, diagrams and plans, to high-quality lined paper for final drafts. Collecting this range need not be expensive: you can make good use of old envelopes, backs of old Christmas cards, self-adhesive notes that teachers and parents have kept from the trade shows and exhibitions they have visited. Everyone can help out and nothing should be wasted.

The paper children use and the implements they use to write with can have a profound effect not just on the confidence with which they write, but also on the type of writing that they produce. If they are given self-adhesive notes, for example, they know from the outset that they are not expected to write at length and by their very nature these notes encourage quick and spontaneous ideas that we can move around and rearrange. Similarly, scrap paper signals quick ideas without getting anxious about spelling or carefully formed letters. Big, chunky pens say record your ideas together so that everyone can see them – the importance of these choices cannot be overemphasised. The range needs to be readily accessible and children should be encouraged to make thoughtful decisions about what they will use and when. It is always tempting to make these choices for children, often in the name of getting on quickly, but real writers make choices about both what and how they write.

Writers' notebooks

Many writers have these – books in which they keep jottings, ideas, observations, drawings and cuttings. It is worth investing in good-quality books with, if possible, hard covers. Children may keep these from one school year to the next so that they build up into a bank of thoughts, observations and ideas. They need not be anything that teachers mark or even look in, unless asked to do so by the writer. In one project with which we were involved, these notebooks had a quite dramatic impact on children's attitudes to writing. They kept them close to hand and used them in all sorts of settings and situations. Most significantly though, they told us that the notebooks were an important part of what made them feel like real writers.

Message boxes

This is another idea that we can borrow from the best early years practice. Each child has a message box and these are used for a wide variety of communication directly between children. They can be made quite easily – shoe boxes would do to start with. However, once the children are using them regularly, you will probably want to invest in something more durable and your local DIY store will be full of all sorts of reasonably priced possibilities.

Clearly it is important that the ground rules for these are established from the outset – like any form of communication, electronic or otherwise, it can be used for good or ill. When they are used well, children enjoy sending each other all sorts of messages: news about what they have been doing outside school, cards and greetings, invitations to a party or even just to join a game at playtime. Whatever the message, it involves writing for a real and meaningful purpose.

News desks and bulletin boards

In many primary school classrooms, the start of the day is characterised by children vying for the teacher's attention with news about their lives outside school. It might be about a visit they have been on, a medal or certificate they have won, some domestic news, even the birth of a baby brother or sister. A news desk and/or bulletin board should be in a prominent and accessible place in the classroom. It can be accessed and added to by children, teachers, parents, governors and other members of the school community. It may include photographs and objects that have been brought in, but they will all be supported and explained by writing. You may want to include a cassette tape recorder or simple digital voice recorder so that some children can record their news for others to play back. Like any new idea in the classroom, you will need to be very persistent, particularly when introducing it in the first place: if the board is not kept up to date it will achieve nothing and may even have a detrimental effect.

Working walls

At its best, the 'working wall' is a valuable resource that supports children at all stages of the writing process. It will be covered with notes and ideas that children have gathered and recorded through the sorts of structures and activities that we use throughout this book. It will also have tips and ideas to help with spelling, vocabulary, sentence and text structures. The best of these will be produced by the children themselves: results of spelling investigations; posters and annotated examples of texts; mnemonics that they have devised for spelling, etc. Ideas that have grown from the children's own experiences and practice as writers are infinitely more valuable – and much more likely to be noticed and used – than any number of commercially produced posters or carefully laminated targets and exhortations.

Displays of work in progress

These can be a really good way of recognising and celebrating that good writing comes about through a variety of processes. As well as displaying children's writing at various stages of its development, the display might also include photographs of children at work, and drawings and notes they have made along the way.

Finished and published work

In the writing classroom, examples of children's finished work are widely available. Some will be displayed on the wall, but there will also be books that have been created with anthologies of children's writing as well as individual children's work in the form of home-made books, magazines and comics. This need not be limited to the children who are in the class at the time, but may include work that other children did when they were in that class, or maybe writing that has been specially commissioned from older children in the school. The richer the variety of children's own writing that is available, the more it emphasises that, in this classroom, children are thought of and treated like writers. A good range of children's work also offers plenty of models of writing to which other children can realistically aspire.

Flexible spaces

Another characteristic of the writing classroom is that it can be used in a variety of ways. Of course this is very much easier to achieve in some settings than in others, but even if your classroom is not large enough to have specific areas that are set aside for particular ways of working, you and your class can collaborate to think about how you can change it and use it as flexibly as possible. How quickly and quietly can the children move desks and tables to one side to create a space for walking, talking and active writing? If we need a time where we can all work and write quietly for a sustained period, what is the best way to arrange the room? If you can encourage children to tackle these problems with you, they are much more likely to invest in and abide by the agreements that you all make. Of course there will be compromises: not all writers like to work in the same way. But the more inventive we can be about using our classroom flexibly, the more likely it will be that we will meet most writers' needs.

Building a culture of writing in the classroom

The well-resourced and well-organised classroom that we outline will make a significant contribution to developing a positive attitude to writing in children and a growing sense of themselves as writers. Yet, however carefully chosen and well used the resources, we still need to take deliberate and careful steps to foster and maintain that sense. Building such a culture is not something that can be done quickly and, as we shall explore shortly, it is very much more effective if some of these steps are taken as a whole school. But even if you feel you are a lone teacher trying to bring about a 'writing culture' in your own classroom, there is much that you can do. Once others start to see the effects, they will quickly become interested in what you do and want to learn more.

A culture of talk

It seems almost too obvious to say that writing is built on talk, but the importance of valuing and deliberately developing spoken language in young writers cannot be overemphasised. So many of the approaches we illustrate throughout the book begin with activities to generate talk. In recent years many teachers have become very familiar with a range of strategies for structuring speaking and listening in their classrooms; from jigsaw groups to barrier games to drama conventions like 'Conscience alley'. These are all valuable strategies that can be harnessed right across the curriculum, but they must be underpinned by a central principle: that we welcome and value what *all* children have to say. If a child feels that no one wants to hear her words, why would she ever bother to write them down?

As everyone knows through their everyday social conversations with friends, talk leads to talk. You talk, I respond, and so our conversation develops a life of its own. And as we do that, we learn from each other – we might pick up vocabulary and patterns of speech, but we also hear and reflect on each other's experiences, views and opinions. So the writing classroom is also a talking classroom where we learn when and how to speak, when to listen, how and when to build on the ideas of others, how and when to challenge them. Of course managing talk with 30 excitable young people is challenging, and the manner and volume of their talk can all too easily become a battleground between children and their teachers. But to deal with the difficulty by suppressing talk is a dangerous way to go – if talk, learning and writing are so closely linked, then the predominantly silent classroom is a chilling place to be.

A culture of story

If you go into a staffroom on the first morning back after a holiday, it will be filled with talk. And if you take a moment to listen to all those noisy conversations, you will probably find that what is going on is 'storying' – so much of what is said is in the form of a story. Those stories will mostly be about what has happened since people last met: the trip abroad; the sick relative; the broken washing machine. In creating these everyday tales, we edit and recast our experiences into forms that we hope will interest, entertain or amuse others. Sometimes we might elaborate and invent to make our stories more exciting, sometimes we might shape them to reflect better on us, sometimes we might humbly play down the importance or bravery of what we did. However we choose to tell them, that shaping of experience into a compelling story is fundamental to the writer's craft. So the writing classroom is also a storytelling classroom.

It might be argued that there is little point in children writing stories in school because most of what they will have to write in their adult lives will be non-fiction. This view is deeply misguided. Firstly, it underestimates how much writing is essentially narrative in form: the irate letter one of us had to write to the local council about our rubbish collection might be classified as non-fiction, but it was essentially a narrative account of events; and instructions might be thought of as the 'story' of how to do or achieve something. Secondly, it fails to recognise the connection between stories and imagination: they tell not only of how things were or are, but how they *might* be. Unless children can invent stories of how their world *could* or *might* be different, they are stuck with it the way it is. Storytelling is indispensable in developing imagination, creativity, ingenuity and invention. And thirdly, stories are sources for the most joyful sharing and celebrating in our classrooms: they bind us together and celebrate our common humanity.

The writing classroom welcomes and celebrates stories of all sorts. From jokes and anecdotes, to folk-tales and fairy-tales, to creation stories that tell how the world came to be. Stories are read, written and told. The skills of the oral storyteller are immensely valuable for teachers and young writers alike. Few storytellers remember their stories word for word, rather they hold the overall structure of it in their heads, extemporising and elaborating as they go. If you tell a story, you get direct and immediate feedback from your audience; you learn how to hold their attention, how to tease and build tension, how to make them smile, laugh or cry – all fundamental for the skilled writer. If a teacher shows the willingness and commitment to develop and use these skills herself, the children will soon want to follow. You can enhance this storytelling culture by having a special storyteller's chair, perhaps also getting a class 'story stick' (an old walking stick will do very well) that the storyteller holds to tell his tale.

A culture of writing for change

In the writing classroom children understand that writing can be a very powerful way to change things for the better. *Click, Clack, Moo*, one of the stories we referred to in Chapter 3, is a splendid illustration of this: once the cows have mastered the written word, they use it to better their conditions. In the writing classroom this immediate power may start with message boxes and news boards through which writing helps children to make and maintain all sorts of social connections. We might also write letters to the headteacher, or perhaps to the governors of the school, making a case and asking for new equipment or changes to the school day. If we want to change things, the pen is often the first thing for which we reach.

A culture of publication

The word 'publication' can seem rather formal, even intimidating. But if we think of it as making our work public by putting it into forms where others can read it, it quickly becomes a much more accessible and everyday process in all classrooms. Displaying children's writing on the walls is commonplace but, as we have already suggested, the means by which children can publish their work go well beyond that. Whether it is through making their own books, sharing their work electronically, or writing for the school magazine or community newsletter, children expect publication to be a natural part of life in the writing classroom and rise to the challenge eagerly.

A culture of collaboration

Many of the strategies we have illustrated throughout this book involve working in pairs, groups and with the whole class to generate ideas and vocabulary to support the writing process. By working and sharing together, we build a resource that is available to all of us in the later stages of our writing. Not least because of the way we test children as individuals, it is tempting to believe that writing should always be done alone. As we explored in Chapter 6 though, many forms of writing result from collaboration between people – this book is an example in itself and, though there are times when each of us sits alone and writes, it is also the result of lots of conversation, shared planning, revising and editing. Friends, family and colleagues help out by reading and commenting on drafts, and the teaching practices it describes result from years of collaboration with colleagues and children in all sorts of settings. In the writing classroom 'my writing' is also 'our writing'. We deliberately build a community where we share and borrow ideas from each other, where to be copied is taken as a compliment rather than an affront, and where we all delight in the success of everyone.

A culture of positive criticism

Young writers in the writing classroom all want to improve. They see this in a very positive way and know how to give and receive constructive criticism. Knowing how that is done needs to start with the teacher, and we showed in Chapter 7 how the best marking and responding to children's work can help build a culture in which everyone enjoys contributing to the process of refinement and improvement. The process will begin by pointing out not only *what* is good but *why* it is good. We can deliberately teach children how to use phrases like:

- I love this sentence because . . .
- I think **** is a very thoughtful choice of word because . . .
- That section of dialogue made your characters seem very real.
- I was really excited at this point and I couldn't wait to find out what happened next.
- The way you wrote this section made me feel like I was right there with them.

If children hear their teachers using phrases like these, they will quickly pick them up and use them. Of course, young writers also need to know how their writing can be improved, but they are much more likely to accept suggestions from teachers or peers if they are made in a culture of support and celebration of what is good. Again, the language used to explore improvements needs to be carefully phrased:

- I wonder if **** might be a better word here?
- What would the effect be if we were to join those two sentences into one?
- How about starting a new paragraph here, to make it clear we have moved on?

The phrasing of these as questions is very deliberate, but children will very quickly realise if questions are just thinly disguised suggestions or instructions. In the writing classroom, children learn that it is good to respond to the suggestions of others and justify why they made certain choices. If a teacher or peer is sometimes prepared to listen and then say, 'Do you know, I think you're right – stick with your original idea', it can help to strengthen a sense that we are in a real writer's conversation and so build confidence.

A culture of shared ambition

In the writing classroom, most of the drive and desire for improvement comes from the children themselves. This is a very different culture from one that relies primarily on targets that are imposed from outside. Of course children need to know how to get better, how to be very specific about the improvements they need to make, and how to recognise when they have got there. But those expectations and ambitions need to be expressed in language which they can readily understand and embrace. This can only come about by carefully and critically reading what young writers write, engaging in meaningful conversations with them about their writing, and agreeing with them what individuals, groups and the whole class should focus on as their next areas for development. Once decided, it can be very helpful to write these ambitions down in language that is clear and accessible to the children so that they can remind themselves what they are aiming to do. But this approach is very different from lifting targets from an external source, typing and laminating them, and then hanging them over children's seats like the Sword of Damocles. The writing classroom is filled with ambition, but that ambition comes from within the children.

Stepping back and letting go

Writers need time to write, and few of them can work effectively by grabbing a few moments here and there to add a couple more sentences. They need sustained and uninterrupted periods where they can establish and maintain momentum in their writing. All the time, effort and energy we put into the writing process with children needs ultimately to result in them spending an extended period writing. There are no readily available formulae for this – it will depend on the ages, ability and preferences of particular classes and groups. Effective teachers negotiate these extended writing sessions with their classes: what particular outcomes we are all looking for; how long the session(s) should be; and how the room should be arranged. Then children need the space and time to write and write and write.

Building a culture of writing across the whole school

Many of the approaches we outline for the writing classroom are directly applicable across the whole school. In particular, the elements that stress publication and shared celebration can readily spread beyond the classroom. When you walk into a 'writing school' the evidence of children's engagement with and excitement about the written word is everywhere: in displays on the walls; in all sorts of publications, some of which are electronic; children's work is regularly read and applauded in assemblies and other school events; when an author visits he is welcomed as a fellow rather than revered as a celebrity. This sense of a community of writers is supported by a number of opportunities and practices.

Magazines, newsletters and other periodicals

Most schools would expect to send out regular newsletters to parents informing them about upcoming events and other matters of concern or interest. These can readily be adapted to offer more opportunities for children's writing to be included. They might want to inform parents about work they have been doing, ask for help with an event they are planning, or perhaps ask for resources and ideas for a project they are planning.

What is most important is that they see this kind of local publication as an effective means of communicating with a particular audience for a particular purpose.

Many schools also produce a regular magazine which might include articles by children about a particular hobby or interest, reports of visits or work in school, short stories and poems, cartoon strips, games and puzzles, perhaps even a problem page. The technology that is now widely available in schools makes it possible to produce these to a much higher and more professional standard than was possible just a few years ago – you may even be lucky enough to have parents who work in the publishing or printing industries and are willing to offer help and advice. At their best these magazines have an editorial board or group drawn from the children, who are provided with advice and support by a committed teacher.

Then there may be publications that appear once or twice a year and contain anthologies of children's work which include poetry, short stories and non-fiction. They represent a variety of work from across the age range and allow children to see their work published in more lasting ways. Of course, all of these forms of publication have cost implications but these can be offset either by making a small charge for them or perhaps by seeking sponsorship from local businesses and other organisations.

The school website

Most primary schools now have a website of some kind. It may be used primarily to provide information about the school, its location and other contextual information, performance data, information about staffing, etc. But the best sites also include plenty of children's input and examples of their work. As we explored in Chapter 6, this represents an opportunity to publish to the whole world. It can be particularly powerful where children have friends and family who live far from their school because, even if they cannot visit in person, they can still see and celebrate a child's published work. As we also stressed in Chapter 6, children need thoughtful support and guidance in how they present their work in these media so that they can explore how its presentation affects how it is read on screen.

Celebrating writing

The publication possibilities we have discussed throughout this chapter can have a terrific impact on a child's sense of herself as a writer, making her feel that her work is of genuine value and interest to others and so building her confidence and desire to write more. This willingness to value and celebrate children's work can be apparent in many areas of school life. When work is publicly displayed it is always with the care and attention that it deserves. If it is read aloud either in a classroom or an assembly, it has been properly read through and rehearsed beforehand. The status and impact of a child's writing can be dramatically enhanced if it is read professionally by a teacher or another adult, but only if they have taken care to familiarise themselves with it so that the reading makes the writing sound fluid and coherent – even if that fluidity and coherence is not evident at first reading. Of course children should be encouraged to read their own writing aloud too, but we need to be sensitive to those who might find this difficult, uncomfortable or embarrassing. As we have stressed throughout, the best writing is often highly personal and it can take considerable courage to share it: we often notice how few adults are willing to do so on courses and we would never think of insisting.

Almost all primary schools have sports days, regular matches where their teams play other schools, and performances and concerts throughout the year. These events mirror the cultural and sporting events that take place in the wider world. So how might we celebrate writing in the same way? There are a number of literary festivals internationally, nationally and locally. Writers attend to read and talk about their work, panels discuss new work and trends in writing, there are talks about particular authors, and there are book signings. What is so joyful about these occasions is that people come together with a shared love of the written word. An event like this in school might start on a very small scale, perhaps with just one class taking the lead. They can plan events and readings, prepare publications for sale, organise food and drink, perhaps include some live music. It may just be one afternoon in the school hall to which their parents and children from other classes are invited. It is important though that it doesn't just become an event where too many people are crammed into the hall and a succession of children stand up and read their work. It is much more effective if there are number of shorter events that take place in different spaces at different times, and it can actually be rather a good thing if there is a heavy demand for tickets and some events are sold out. In one school, staff and children organised a writers' festival in the summer and made wonderfully imaginative use of the grounds. They borrowed tents and gazebos and made use of naturally shaded spaces for children to read, share and have their work celebrated and applauded by the whole school community.

Writers talking to writers

Lots of professional writers, particularly those who write for children, like to visit schools to talk and work with young writers. Many of the best-known authors continue to dedicate a good deal of their time to this and it can be quite thrilling for children to meet people whose names they have seen only on the covers of their books. But they are much in demand and arranging a visit from one can be a challenge. If you are lucky enough to secure a visit, it is well worth spending time to prepare for it. What questions will the children have? How will asking those questions help the children as writers? What of their work would they like to share with a fellow author and how? How can they make sure everyone gets the most they can from the visit? Young writers will get so much more from a visit that has been thoughtfully planned than they will from being crammed into a hall, asked to listen to a reading or two, and then expected to come up with questions spontaneously.

It need not just be names with a national profile that come into school to talk about their writing. A little research will quickly turn up local writers, some of whom write professionally or semi-professionally. Journalists on local papers, those who contribute regularly to local magazines and newsletters, other people who write regularly as part of their job – all will have a perspective to share with children and can be welcomed into school as fellow writers.

Connecting with the community

Once a culture of writing and writers is established in your classrooms and is beginning to grow across the whole school, you will find it a natural progression to reach out and connect with the wider community. As this happens, the barriers between younger and older writers begin to break down and your school becomes the hub for writing in the whole community. Why should a school magazine be kept exclusively for children's writing? Why can't children's poems and short stories be published in an anthology that includes the work of teachers and other adults in the community? In one example an older member of the community had published her recollections of rationing after World War II alongside a child's poem about wartime evacuation. Once people in the community realise that they can be included, you will be surprised by the numbers of people who are willing to come forward and offer help. And it needn't stop at paper publications: there can be equally strong links between community websites and schools. The writing community and the community as a whole grow together.

Once these initiatives take hold, children find themselves in a community that has writing embedded in its very fabric. Writing is something that everyone does and it connects people in just the same way as talk, music, song and dance – it is a vital part of what makes us who we are. Such a view of writing does not pursue the notion of 'high standards' as an end in itself, it embraces high standards as necessary to make writing good. The young writers who are part of this community do not learn to write only because they will need the skills when they are older, they write because they love to and because they simply have to. Above all, they write because they are writers.

Appendix 1

Strategies, games and activities used throughout the book

Objects and experts

Children use self-adhesive notes to scribble down as many questions as they can about an unusual object, then one takes the role of the 'expert'. An excellent game to encourage deeper thinking and creative problem solving. (Page 16)

Make me a . . .

This is a game that requires children to collaborate and use their imagination. In large or small groups, they silently form the shape of whatever the leader might choose. It could be a full stop, a question mark, or an enchanted tree. (Page 17)

The noticing game

A quick and entertaining outdoor activity, where children walk around in a space, close their eyes and then point to the features the teacher calls out. The object of the exercise is to see how much they have noticed in their immediate environment. (Page 18)

Bringing the outdoors in

Children walk into an interesting space and take it back to the classroom in the form of words. They collect words for textures, sounds and things that they have seen. (Page 19)

Word carpet

After investigating a setting or a soundscape, children write words and descriptions on individual pieces of paper, using chunky pens. They lay the words and phrases across the floor, organising them like a map, thinking carefully about their position. (Page 20)

Hide, write and seek

A simple game that makes reading and writing active and enjoyable. Groups hide puppets or other objects from each other and provide a written set of clues to guide them to the right place. (Page 22)

Scavenger hunt

Children are given a list of unusual objects to find. Rather than returning with the objects, they can only return with words. This is quick, enjoyable and encourages children to be descriptive and imaginative. (Page 23)

Nightline

An outward bound-style activity that involves moving through an obstacle course in the dark. The sensations that children experience help them to develop their language skills. (Page 25)

Book bingo

A quick speaking and listening activity. Children move around the room and when prompted, find a partner and chat about books they have read. When they find one in common they shout 'bingo!' (Page 34)

Book web

Children sit in a circle, each with a book they have read in front of them. As they make connections between their books, they roll a ball of wool across the circle until they have made a huge web of connections. (Page 34)

There's a book over there that . . .

Children form groups of about four. Starting from these groups, they move among a collection of books. On a signal from the teacher they go to a particular book and find out as much as they can about it in a short time. Then they return to their group and feed back before moving to look at the books again following what they have heard. (Page 34)

Play and freeze

A simple drama strategy for young children in which they free play at being characters in a story and 'freeze' or 'still' on a given signal. (Page 51)

Still images/tableaux/freeze frames

Children work in pairs or groups to capture a moment in time as if standing in a photograph or painting. Those standing back from the image can explore the complexities of character and narrative. (Page 57)

Still – move – still

When children are asked to produce a series of still frames, each separate tableau is linked together with carefully chosen movement, sound and/or words. (Page 57)

Soundscapes

After thinking about different features of a setting, children create the landscape using sound, carefully placing their audience to achieve the most dramatic effect. (Page 57)

Listen – call back – write!

This is a useful way to get children to respond to the spoken word in written form. Children listen to spoken language, either being read aloud or recorded on film or radio. When they hear language that stands out to them they call it. At the end of the activity they quickly jot down as many interesting phrases as they can remember. (Page 57)

Making sound symbols

This activity teaches children how to respond to sound in written form. Because symbols are created as a result of individual interpretation the anxiety of 'doing it wrong' is completely removed. This confident mark making is a first step to confident writing of words. (Page 63)

Sound story

Children listen carefully to the sounds they can hear in their own environment. They create sounds that tell the individual story of the room they are in. (Page 65)

Change the sound

This activity enhances children's noticing skills. They have to tune in to sound and movement and eventually find their own language to describe the sounds they hear. (Page 69)

Word orchestra

Children use descriptive language to express different sounds they have heard. When the conductor points to them, they whisper, speak or shout their phrases. Words are layered over words in an improvised poem. (Page 72)

Catching a picture in your hand

An image is projected from an overhead projector into the corner of the room. The distorted picture can only be seen by catching fragments of it on blank paper which the children hold up to the light. (Page 73)

Stepping into an image

A picture is projected as large as possible on to an empty wall. Children step into the picture as though they were there when the image was captured. (Page 75)

Message boxes

Every child in the classroom has their own box with their name on. All children in the class are encouraged to write messages to each other to post in the boxes. (Page 114)

News desks and bulletin boards

These invite children to share information about themselves with the rest of the class. Their short written descriptions are changed regularly so that the boards work as an interactive display. (Page 115)

Appendix 2

The version of 'The Elves and the Shoemaker' used in Chapter 4

Once upon a time there was an old man. He lived with his wife and the two of them were very poor. They had not always been poor, for the old man was a shoemaker, and once he had been a very fine shoemaker indeed. When he was doing his best work, everyone agreed he was the finest shoemaker in the district, some thought him the best shoemaker in the land, and one or two wondered if perhaps he was the best shoemaker in all the world.

But as he grew older the shoemaker found it harder and harder to see his work. To begin with he made only the tiniest of mistakes and you would have needed to be as fine a shoemaker as he to find them. As his eyes grew worse and worse though, he made bigger and bigger mistakes. Soon no one wanted his shoes and no one came to his shop and he and his wife just grew poorer and poorer.

One day the old man's wife looked in the jar where they kept their money and said, 'My husband we have very little money left. When this is gone I don't know what will become of us.' The old man took up the jar, tipped it out on their table, and counted the money. 'Do you know,' he said, 'I think there may be just enough money left to buy the leather to make one last pair of shoes. I will work slowly and carefully and try to make the best shoes I can. If we can sell those, we may make enough money to buy leather for two pairs of shoes. Then perhaps we can make a new start.'

The old woman was not at all keen on his idea but what else could they do? So she gave him all their money and he went off and bought the leather. He had just enough money left over to buy half a loaf of dry bread for their supper.

As soon as he got back, the old man set to work. But it was already late and it quickly grew too dark for him to see, so he left the shoes unfinished on his bench. He and his wife ate their dry bread, drank some water and went off to bed.

Next morning the old man got up as soon as it was light, so keen was he to get on with his work. He went to his bench and was quite amazed by the sight that greeted him: for there on the bench was a perfectly finished pair of shoes. As far as his old eyes could see they were perfect in every detail, but it was only when he ran his old fingers over the stitching that he realised just how fine the work was. He went straight to the shop window to put the shoes on show.

By and by a customer came in. He tried on the shoes and they fitted perfectly. Quite delighted, the customer reached into his pocket, paid the old man and all but danced out of the shop. 'Look!' the old man called to his wife. 'Now we have enough money for leather to make two pairs of shoes!' And off he went into town. That day, after buying his leather, he had enough money left over to buy a whole loaf of bread and even a little jam to go with it. He sat and worked at his bench all afternoon, but still the shoes were not finished before dark. So they ate their bread and jam and went off to bed.

The next morning not one but two pairs of finished shoes lay waiting on his bench, just as fine as the first. He put them in the window and by and by two customers came by. Now here is a very strange thing: the first customer was very tall with very large feet and the shoes he tried on fitted perfectly; the second had very small feet but her shoes still fitted like gloves. Both were quite delighted. They paid the shoemaker and skipped out of the shop to show off their lovely new shoes. The shoemaker knew that he now had enough money to buy the leather to make four pairs of shoes. And for supper that night they had bread, jam and even cheese! Once again, though, he could not finish his work before dark.

And you can guess what happened the next morning – four pairs of beautifully stitched shoes on his work bench. He didn't have to wait for customers because when he went to the door there was a queue. 'Only the first four please!' he called. 'The rest of you will have to try again tomorrow.' And do you know, it didn't matter if the customer was tall or short or fat or thin, the shoes always seemed to fit just perfectly.

And so it went: each day there were more pairs of shoes and each day more money for leather. There was more money for food too and as the days went by the old man and his wife enjoyed better and better suppers.

Now I don't know if you've ever done this, but if you eat too much too late it can be very difficult to sleep. That is what happened to the old man one night: he was so full that try as he might, he could not get to sleep. And it was while he lay there trying to get comfortable that he heard the most peculiar sound coming from his workshop. He got out of bed, lit his candle, and quietly made his way to the top of the stairs that led down to his workshop. Very slowly, he crept down the stairs to see if he could find where the noise was coming from. And when he got to his workshop even his old eyes could make out the most amazing sight they had ever seen. Do you know what he saw?

Index